Testimonials

"Paul and Emer's track record of helping companies close the growth gap, ... , ... If you're seeking faster growth in your business, this immensely pragmatic book will give you the toolkit you need to take your business where you want it to go".

John Mullins, Associate Professor of Management Practice, London Business School (Author: The Customer-Funded Business and, co-author with Randy Komisar, Getting to Plan-B)

"Scaling a business globally is hard. The challenges are complex and varied, whether they are related to market, product or building your team. The insightful approach to scaling outlined in The Growth Roadmap® really helped Fenergo focus on what matters to take us to the next level".

Marc Murphy, Founder & CEO, Fenergo

"The Growth Roadmap® aligned our team around an ambitious strategy. It helped our team dig deep into the business and make key decisions that accelerated scale".

Barry Napier, CEO, Cubic Telecom

"The Growth Roadmap® will push its reader to think about their growth gap in a new and inspiring manner. Through insightful examples and a clear roadmap the book provides a framework to help any ambitious organisation unlock its potential for change and success".

Timothy Houstoun, CEO, Global Shares

"Working through the process was a game changer for us. It led to a shift in the ambition of the team. We set our sights way higher than before. We came through with a clear execution plan to grow the business globally".

David Walsh, Founder & CEO, Netwatch

Testimonials

"Scaling and realising your brand's potential is only possible through disruptive thinking and a scaling mindset. The Growth Roadmap® provides the tools and frameworks to enable you and your leadership team realise the potential of your company, product and culture. Importantly our customers are being delivered more value as a result – that is quite simply what it is all about".

Mark Barrett, Co-Founder & CEO APC (The Applied Process Company)

"The process was very useful for our senior leadership team. After doubling the business over three years, we needed help with the next phase of growth. The Growth Roadmap® showed us a clear path we were not seeing. This enabled us to make better choices and become more aligned, putting us on a course to continue scaling the business".

Ronan Stafford, CEO, Codec

"Our senior leadership team has worked with the authors to successfully address various challenges as we've scaled. I would highly recommend the framework provided in this book to other founders seeking scale – it is a proven model".

John Beckett, Founder & CEO, ChannelSight

"When it came to building our 2020 scaling plan we went straight to Select Strategies. Twenty five team members, a clear framework and two intense workshops later we had the essence of our scaling plan for the next three years. We have revised and updated that plan since, but the core remains and still drives the business today".

Leo Corcoran, Founder & CEO, ClaimVantage, Portland, Maine, USA

"The Growth Roadmap® is a practical and timely book that clearly outlines the stages of growth management in a global context. It also describes important aspects of strategy execution. I particularly liked the authors' advice on how to develop a personalised scaling scorecard. Reading this book is a good use of time for every entrepreneur and manager in a growing company".

Professor Walter Kuemmerle, President, Kuemmerle Research Group, Ltd., former professor Harvard Business School

Testimonials

"If only I had read this 30 years ago. This book is a practical insightful step-by-step guide to scaling a business with practical advice on the logical gates an ambitious company needs to navigate. Like previous books the authors have once again knocked it out of the park".

John Purdy, Founder & CEO, Ergo Group

"This book should be read, not only by every CEO of ambitious and growth-focused companies, but also by anyone who is a member of such firms management team, board or anyone who has invested in them. The authors do a brilliant job of bringing the most typical growth pains and barriers alive with insightful examples and then guiding the reader through a clear path of analysing, defining and executing a successful growth strategy".

Marc Sosna, Director of Learning Innovation Unit, IESE Business School, Barcelona

"The journey we went on from diagnosis through to strategy and execution was significant. The process helped our team identify the growth gaps we needed to address and led to important decisions. Now we have an ambitious roadmap to scale that our international team is focused on delivering".

Jan Patrick Schultz, CEO, Landbell Group, Germany

"Getting your internationally based team aligned and on the same page is always a challenge. The Growth Roadmap® gave us a framework to help the team debate and discuss our strategic direction. Ultimately allowing us to make choices and get commitment from the whole team".

Peter Cosgrove, CEO, ATA Group

Published by

Oak Tree Press, Cork T12 EVTO, Ireland

www.SuccessStore.com

© 2020 Paul O'Dea & Emer O'Donnell.

A catalogue record of this book is available from the British Library.

ISBN 978-1-78119-450-8 – Paperback

ISBN 978-1-78119-451-5 – ePub

ISBN 978-1-78119-452-2 – Kindle

ISBN 978-1-78119-453-9 – PDF

The Growth Roadmap® is a registered trademark of Select Strategies Limited.

Design by hexhibit.com

Acknowledgements

Many people, senior leadership teams, advisors and academics have influenced the content in this book, none more so than the CEOs of growing companies that we have had the privilege of working with over the past two decades. Their challenges, stories and experiences have guided us throughout to focus on delivering a book that is 'practical and usable'.

We are particularly grateful to the 60 or so clients who have participated in what we call the Growth Roadmap® process. We continually learned from them. Each has had their own unique opportunities and challenges. Many have faced disruption themselves or were disrupting others. Disruption is dynamic and can come from many sources – technological, political or economic. Our aim has always been to provide a practical guide to steer our clients through regardless.

In writing this book we have drawn on a wide spectrum of thinking. From the academic business schools of Stanford, Harvard, IESE and Cambridge, to leading consultancies such as Bain, McKinsey and Bath Consulting group, all have contributed to our understanding and to the work we do with our clients. Enterprise Ireland, a long-time partner and supporter of growth businesses, has also had a significant influence on our approach.

We are especially grateful to all those who reviewed early drafts and whose honest feedback and encouragement made this a better book – Dennis Barnedt, Grant Kinsman, Donnchadh Kavanagh, Terry McWade, Brian Rowan and Lisa Vaughan.

A special thanks to Katie O'Dea, Brian O'Kane and Pat Scully whose work on the early drafts helped clarify and hone our thinking. Particular thanks to Bridget Hourican, who once again has proven to be a great and patient editor – we cannot recommend her highly enough. She improved the book's flow and content greatly. And of course, sincere thanks to Alastair Keady whose insightful approach produced the visual language and graphics that support the key messages of the book.

A huge thanks to Sean Ellis, for inspiring us and countless ambitious companies across the globe. Your scientific approach to growth, in companies such as Dropbox, Eventbrite and LogMeIn, has been influential in our thinking. Sincere thanks also for writing the *Foreword* for our book.

Putting together a book like this is beyond the capability of the authors alone. We have had the opportunity and privilege of testing and refining the concepts and tools with a terrific (and patient) cadre of CEOs and management teams. Each engagement has refined the framework and we hope this book does their input justice.

Throughout the book we share the experiences of clients, whom we have disguised for confidentiality reasons. We thank those clients who have generously allowed us to share their stories. We hope their journeys inspire and inform yours.

And finally to our families, editors-in-chief Clare and Rory, who pushed us through the final hurdle and who provided us with unfailing support and encouragement. To the future generation Sean, Maria, Ross, Owen and Cara – the book is finally finished and we hope one day you will find some inspiration in our writings.

I have always been intrigued by company growth challenges, particularly ones where the odds are tough, like fierce competition and clients with tight growth budgets. Whether it was the early stages of Dropbox with Drew Houston or companies like Uproar or LogMeIn, I was fortunate enough to discover novel ways to find, reach and learn from customers, in order to scale sales and marketing.

Over time, I refined and codified these growth tactics. By rapidly testing and evaluating them according to objective metrics, this approach enabled faster discovery of which ideas were viable, and which should be dismissed. In 2010, I coined the term 'growth hacking' to describe the approach of acquiring lots of customers fast using modest budgets. Whilst the approach has become an umbrella term, I along with Morgan Brown codified the process in our best selling book **Hacking Growth: *How today's fastest-growing companies drive breakout success.***

There is no doubt that stalled growth is one of the most pernicious and pressing problems for today's businesses. The challenges that face companies seeking to scale internationally are well understood but are nevertheless difficult to overcome. All too often companies get caught in the day-to-day and fail to achieve their true potential. And as the world becomes more complex, and business changes at an even faster pace, there is a risk that even more companies will fall at this hurdle.

I first met Paul and Emer eight years ago when we worked together on a growth acceleration programme for internet and games companies – iGAP. A shared determination to help companies of all kinds achieve their potential kept us in touch since. I am delighted that Paul and Emer have taken the opportunity to codify and share their experience in their new book.

In The Growth Roadmap® they provide ambitious senior leadership teams with a proven framework to achieve their potential. Built on the back of their research this proven methodology gives teams the path out of the day-to-day and drives them to focus on the strategically important, rather than the urgent. Moreover, it is a method that is repeatable, providing a common language that gets everyone on the team aligned and moving in the same direction.

The Growth Roadmap® speaks a language very much aligned with those of us in the growth hacking community. It focuses on a scientific methodology, seeking data and evidence to diagnose, defining clear scaling challenges and using learning and experimentation to make progress.

I trust that in The Growth Roadmap® you will find a framework to help you and your team on the path to scale.

Sean Ellis

Sean is an entrepreneur and investor, who coined the phrase 'growth hacking' after using it to ignite breakout growth for Dropbox, LogMeIn and Eventbrite.

CONTENTS

Introduction   5

    The Growth Roadmap®   8

Stage 1: Uncover Diagnosis   **15**

    Gathering Data for the Diagnosis   20

    Four Company Areas: Market,
    Product, Leadership & Performance   21

    Growth Diagnosis Statement   **34**

Stage 2: Commit to a Shared Vision   35

    Defining your Company Purpose   42

    Setting Stretch Goals   45

    Shifting the Leadership
    Team Mindset   48

    Shared Vision Statement   **53**

Stage 3: Select the Right Strategy   55

    Dual Track – Exploit and Explore   59

    Gaining Industry Insight   63

    Setting Strategic Objectives   65

    Clarifying Product/Market Scope   67

    Creating Competitive Advantage   70

    Strategy Statement   **74**

Stage 4: Overcome Scaling Challenges   **75**

    Selecting your Scaling Challenges   78

    Defining Scaling Challenges   80

    Proposing Solutions   84

    Crafting your Scaling Scorecard   87

    Scaling Scorecard   **88**

Stage 5: Keep Growth on Track   91

    Summary Financial Model   **95**

    **Business Key Performance
    Indicator (KPI) Model**   **99**

    Performance Rhythm   **103**

Conclusion   107

Appendices   113

Worksheets   123

Glossary   131

Introduction

Sitting in the Heathrow airport lounge recently, we struck up a conversation with the Chief Executive Officer (CEO) of a technology company, we'll call him David. No surprise, the conversation quickly steered to business.

David had co-founded his travel focused software company five years previously, and it had achieved significant market growth. He had the kind of passion and energy we've come to associate with good CEOs. He was also clearly frustrated and he wasn't a man to hold back: *"It's as plain as the nose on my face,"* **he told us,** *"growth in the current business is too slow – we have a growth gap".*

"We're making money from about 20% of our customers. We've spent a fortune hiring and have the most talented team we've ever had, but performance is worse. The board are on my case and rightly so. The future market opportunity is massive, but we spend our time firefighting. The market is changing quickly, yet we seem stalled internally and unable to scale".

"We're like a small crew in a rowing boat who made good headway initially but are losing momentum as new crew join and the combined oar strokes lose timing when the weather gets choppy! How do we turn this around? We were good at crossing the sea – maybe we don't have what it takes to navigate the ocean".

With that, David rushed off to catch his next flight to yet another client meeting. With his words ringing in our ears, we couldn't help fearing this meeting would be yet another strenuous oar stroke that wouldn't change direction.

Scaling a company successfully is hard. The team has to keep existing customers happy, while trying to win new customers and see off current competition, all while innovating to stay ahead with future trends. Scaling also requires aligning around vision and purpose, while shifting into the ambitious growth mindset that enables expansion.

Somewhere along this journey all teams run into the choppy waters that David had evoked so well. They feel adrift and misaligned, as if they lack the skills to navigate their environment. Frustration is inevitable because strenuous effort isn't leading to results.

Introduction

Companies can't help but take this personally. They think the problem must lie with them, and like David, they start questioning themselves. Maybe they were only good at start-up and don't have what it takes to scale? Maybe they've made the wrong hires? Does the Chief Technical Officer (CTO) lack vision?

Of course, every company has particular issues which need resolving. But instead of allocating blame, companies can take comfort in the fact that hitting choppy waters is so pervasive that it should be recognised as inherent to the scaling process.

Any business with a strong track record - that has raised funding, developed product and won customers – should be confident that they have what it takes to scale.

But moving from sea to ocean is a huge challenge. The whole climate and environment changes completely. Behaviours and practices that worked in safer, shallower waters are no longer effective. Of course, teams feel overwhelmed and deluged. Of course, they start to flounder, lose confidence in their strengths and abilities, and pull in different directions.

To add to the distress, the opportunity is tantalisingly vast: there's a whole world out there. Frustration is seeing opportunity and not knowing how to grasp it.

We call the shortfall between the team's current performance and its future ambition, the 'growth gap'.

The Growth Gap

A growth gap is a quantifiable gap between the company's current performance and the expectations of the team and investors. It is often expressed in terms of revenue or net profit.

The growth gap develops when companies seek to scale into larger, global markets. It is often indicative of ambition – companies that aren't ambitious don't perceive a gap because they're satisfied with the status quo.

The gap may be particularly noticeable in one area. Perhaps customer service falls obviously short of what's required in the new market or the product is in clear need of a redesign. However, invariably the gap goes across every company area – market, product, leadership and performance – even if this isn't immediately apparent.

If teams leave closing the growth gap to chance or to individual effort, they won't succeed. Individual team members, busy with day-to-day firefighting, will find it impossible to carve out the time.

Because the gap is pervasive, it can only be closed by the whole team stepping back and deciding together a set of company-wide goals and actions during specially scheduled sessions.

Introduction

The Growth Gap

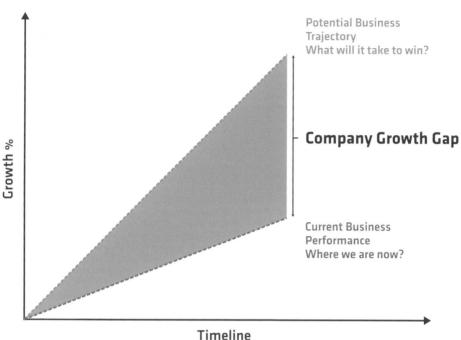

It is best to calculate your Company Growth Gap in the context of your market or competitor growth; and also your stage of development or size. For example, revenue growth at 20% year-on-year might look good but not so good if the market and your competitors are growing at 30% annually. In other contexts it may be better to frame your growth gap in terms of net profit, market share or another relevant growth metric.

The leadership teams of all scaling companies are like David – constantly running to meetings, talking to customers, setting up new prospects, hiring new employees, and answering to a board. They really don't have time to experiment and test things out in a structured and disciplined way.

Firing up the team to close the gap and then stumbling and failing to follow through for lack of a good process, is arguably worse than doing nothing at all. Closing the growth gap tackles both issues that have been holding your company back, and opportunities that can drive it forward to scale successfully.

When the gap seems enormous and non-negotiable, it can help to break the challenge down into clear stages around which the whole team can align.

Introduction

The Growth Roadmap®

Distilled onto one page, The Growth Roadmap® is designed to help your team close the growth gap and scale successfully. It makes scaling growth a continuous process, owned not just by the leadership team but by your whole company.

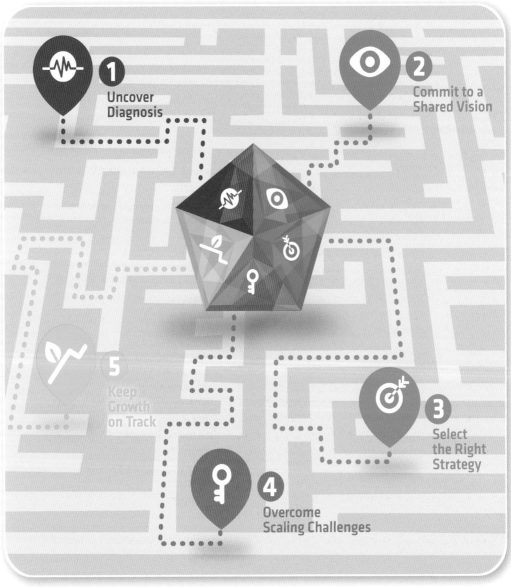

1. Uncover Diagnosis
2. Commit to a Shared Vision
3. Select the Right Strategy
4. Overcome Scaling Challenges
5. Keep Growth on Track

Introduction

The discipline of debating and crafting a growth strategy forces your team to select what's important. The Growth Roadmap® clarifies and aligns your team around a growth strategy. It combines high level strategic principles with a results based approach. It brings growth strategy into the mainstream, rather than leaving it to annual planning sessions, which are often rooted in incremental improvements.

Who We Are

Select Strategies has been advising leadership teams of growth firms on how to scale internationally for over 20 years.

Authors Paul O'Dea and Emer O'Donnell relish the challenge of working with firms seeking to transition to the next phase. We are passionate about helping them succeed. We believe that growth firms have an important role to play in society. They are key contributors to jobs, innovation and wealth in communities. It is our privilege to play a part in helping them realise their vision.

An engineer by profession, Paul has co-founded and scaled several technology-based businesses. He has the scars and the war stories of rapid growth first-hand. Paul is now passionate about figuring out how to scale businesses cost-effectively (helping them avoid some of the mistakes he made)! He is Founder and Managing Director of Select Strategies Limited, which for over two decades have been trusted advisers to CEOs striving to scale their businesses. Paul currently serves on the Boards of several investor-backed businesses and has also had a number of successful exits. He has been a guest speaker at Stanford University and the University of Cambridge. *The Growth Roadmap®* is Paul's third book. His previous books *The Business Battlecard* (2009) and *Select Selling* (2006) have been widely used by entrepreneurs seeking to scale. Paul has served on the Board of Technology Ireland and been an adviser to Enterprise Ireland, Advantage Austria and multiple other organisations on how to scale companies in a repeatable way.

Emer has over two decades experience working with, and as part of, senior leadership teams solving the challenges that come with scaling a business. A Director of Select Strategies, she is specialist in team dynamics and leadership coaching and has led multiple international growth transformation client engagements. A European Mentoring and Coaching Council (EMCC) accredited business coach, Emer is passionate about helping companies unlock and leverage team dynamics to accelerate the delivery of international growth. She has been invited by clients to develop senior team dynamics in their international teams, based in Europe and Asia. Emer is currently programme lead on Enterprise Ireland's start-up initiative Founders Forum (@hpsufoundersforum) and has extensive experience in the delivery of executive education programmes. She is also the author of several industry research reports and publications.

The Growth Roadmap® builds on frameworks published in *The Business Battlecard* (2009) and on our subsequent decade of experience working with clients to help scale their businesses.

Introduction

The Growth Roadmap® – The Five Stages

The Growth Roadmap® provides a common language and approach across the business and works as a catalyst for discussion and dialogue, without making the senior team slaves to a tick-box process.

The Growth Roadmap® breaks the scaling challenge down into five interdependent stages, with the outcomes from each stage impacting the others. Each stage is differentiated by colour and addresses one of the five questions below.

The Growth Roadmap®

Introduction

 Stage 1: Uncover Diagnosis – where are you today?

The first step to addressing the growth gap is identifying what is causing it. Getting to root cause means going beyond superficial symptoms. Good diagnosis is about gathering relevant, targeted data and digging deep into root causes.

 Stage 2: Commit to a Shared Vision – where do you want to get to?

Shared Vision provides the purpose, goals and inspiration that every team needs to succeed. Shared vision connects your team with the core purpose of your business, sets stretch goals that raise ambition, and identifies mindset shifts that will transform growth.

 Stage 3: Select the Right Strategy – how will you get there?

A company's strategy is its plan to win. A good strategy operationalises vision. It is concrete, grounded and specific, providing clear signposts and direction about how the team will leverage existing markets whilst exploring potential new ones.

 Stage 4: Overcome Scaling Challenges – what challenges do you need to address?

Once a team starts implementing its strategy, it will come up against challenges which threaten to prevent scaling, even though the strategy is the right one. Focusing on the critical few things that will enable scaling helps the team to close the growth gap and capitalise on opportunities.

 Stage 5: Keep Growth on Track – how will you ensure that you stick to the plan?

The key to staying focused on delivering growth is to continually monitor progress along the route. What gets measured, gets done. A team that has the right metrics in place and that regularly schedules 'weigh-ins' to check on progress is more likely to stay on track.

For the purposes of this book, the five stages are set out in linear fashion, but our experience is that the reality is more iterative – The Growth Roadmap® balances structure and experimentation. We suggest holding the outcomes from each stage lightly as you go. Nothing is agreed until everything is agreed. You may well find that a decision taken at a 'late' stage affects work done at an earlier stage.

Introduction

Each stage of The Growth Roadmap® has visual tools, charts, worksheets and exercises which draw the whole leadership team into the process to contribute and share ideas. These elements support shared understanding, focus attention and stimulate thinking.

 Questions – for your team to reflect on and think through issues from a company perspective, rather than an individual or departmental one e.g. sales, engineering etc.

 Team exercises – that will help your team debate, induce dialogue and inform decisions, ultimately clarifying direction and commitment.

 Worksheets – to help your team prepare and document ideas for discussion and dialogue. Completed worksheets will make team exercises more profound and productive.

 Statements & Scorecards – that synthesise the work done and become the key pillars of your strategy to scale up.

 Tips – we share short cuts or best practices we have learnt through our work-shops with senior teams that may help your team.

We also include worked examples from the cases we share throughout the book. The work done in each of these elements during The Growth Roadmap® stages is refined into a compelling growth and scaling plan, which can be communicated throughout your company.

Introduction

The Growth Roadmap® – Proven Results

Since 2015, over 60 companies that have adopted The Growth Roadmap® have successfully scaled up and seen 25%+ improvement in performance. This has been achieved through targeting the right market opportunities with the right products and the right leadership approach.

These companies worked methodically through the five stages in order to close the growth gap and successfully compete in larger, global markets. Involving the whole leadership team gave each member ownership of the process and the motivation to keep executing the agreed strategy.

Once all five stages were completed, the companies brought their roadmap to their boards for approval and further insight. The Growth Roadmap® has proven particularly useful for triggering board-level discussions on scale.

Whilst all the leadership teams followed the same framework, each crafted their own individual recipe, suited to their company's particular skills, vision and ambition. We have found that most leadership teams will progress through the stages of the roadmap in 10 – 12 weeks.

Over the past two decades we have spent literally thousands of hours with leadership teams trying to work through their toughest challenges. Inevitably we see patterns repeated, challenges overcome and lessons learnt. We're proud of the success of our clients. Their success is what gives us confidence in The Growth Roadmap® and this fueled our decision to distil our learnings into this publication.

Our Research

In writing this book, we have ensured that our opinions and perspectives are grounded in fact and verifiable data.

To deepen our understanding of the growth gap we conducted in-depth research with over 60 Irish growth firms who had completed The Growth Roadmap®. In addition we surveyed the senior leadership teams of over 250 growth firms and looked at the keys to growth across market, product, leadership and performance.

The companies we researched

The companies we researched typically had revenues of between €2.5m and €100m. Most had between 20 and 250 employees and underlying growth rates of between 10% and 45% per annum.

We looked at a spectrum of companies across a range of sectors and industries – typically founder led, often investor backed, and some family businesses. All had customers in a number of geographies. Many had won major customers through offering disruptive products combined with a persuasive approach. They had seen off bigger competitors who could have provided similar solutions.

What we learned

Our research into these companies confirmed that the growth gap is something that the majority of scaling companies experience. In our research 87% of companies felt that they were in big and growing markets, indicating the capacity for faster growth. Yet only 41% reported that shareholders were satisfied with growth rates and performance. Consistently, leadership teams felt that they could do better, but were constrained by time or experience, to take the right steps.

For readers interested in learning more about our research we have included a summary analysis in Appendix 1.

"Most people spend more time and energy going around problems than in trying to solve them".

HENRY FORD

 Stage 1. Uncover Diagnosis

We first met Peter, the 50 year old CEO of **Aries Solutions**, late one evening. Aries Solutions is a high-end engineering business, delivering products to a range of market segments including financial services, telecoms and industrial waste.

Peter has led the company he originally founded through steady 20% year-on-year growth over the past five years and now employs 150 people. A hands-on CEO and expert in his industry, he enjoys the reputation of an all-rounder. But on our first meeting with him, he was restless and anxious:

"There's something wrong but I can't put my finger on it. Our financial numbers this year look fine at first glance - we're actually a bit ahead of budget, but sales velocity is slowing down. My management team are calling this a blip, but I'm worried about next year's growth. My sales team are blaming new lower cost competitors".

"Some existing customers are telling us they want improved performance from our products, but our engineering team are 15 months behind. One of our bigger customers put a project out to tender, and we nearly lost it on price".

"Something needs to change, but there's so much noise, I don't know which signals to focus on. Should I try to find a new hotshot head of sales? Maybe we need to boost the engineering team to meet demand?"

In our initial diagnostic phase, we talked to all members of Aries' senior team and gathered data using an online survey (see Appendix 2). We then looked for sectoral patterns, comparing Aries' engineering delivery track record to that of similar companies.

We found that, as Peter had said, there was a lot of noise and many signals. Customers in some segments were constantly haggling on price, while in another they were ready to pay a premium but complained that the product wasn't user-friendly.

The CTO was justly renowned for his product expertise but indications were that he wasn't good at discovering customer needs. Meanwhile Peter himself seemed to have 'a finger in every pie' and there were rumbles of discontent over his failure to delegate.

We could see that Aries had got itself a bit stuck. The growth gap between where they currently were and where they wanted to be was widening. All four company areas – market, product, leadership and performance – were now affected. Our initial advice to Peter was to hold off firing or hiring anyone, while we carried out an in-depth diagnosis to uncover the root causes.

Carry out an in-depth diagnosis

When looking for a cause behind success or lack of success, there is always a temptation to take symptoms – like late deliveries – and reach for the most obvious cause, without digging deeper.

This is something we all tend to do – if you have backache, you will probably blame a recent sporting injury and only when you go to the doctor and run tests, do you discover that the sporting injury was actually another symptom and the root cause is something else entirely, perhaps a trapped sciatic nerve.

Getting the right diagnosis for the issues confronting your company is as essential as getting the correct medical diagnosis: you can't apply the cure if you don't know what is causing the problem.

Focus your company diagnosis not just on the present, but on what strategy and actions have taken you to where you are today. In addition to looking at what you said your company would do, look at the patterns and actions that actually happened and question how well these will serve you in the future. Often, what got you here may not be enough to get you where you strive to be.

Stage 1. Uncover Diagnosis

Diagnosis is hard

Good diagnosis is not easy. Companies tend not to have built-in diagnostic processes and teams are naturally consumed with the urgent day-to-day and don't have time to spare.

Diagnosis isn't something the CEO can do alone, no matter how talented and hands-on. Input from the whole senior team is vital in terms of getting overall perspective on the challenges facing the company and, down the line, getting buy-in for execution.

Typically, each member of the team is coming from a different place; with the CEO restless about performance, the head of sales pushing for big deals and the finance team cautious about over-spending. Company reward systems can exacerbate these tendencies – a head of sales rewarded on commissions may be drawn to a different diagnosis than a Chief Financial Officer (CFO) bonused on profit.

If the staff are globally diverse, as is increasingly the case, then language and culture also play a part. In a recent engagement, we found that northern Europeans were more focused on process than their southern European colleagues.

The board and stakeholders add yet another layer. Often politics comes into play, together with differing perspectives on what the company should be. Investors looking for a quick return on investment will take a different view to staff looking for long-term career prospects.

The CEO has perhaps the biggest challenge of all. It's not uncommon for issues to centre around leadership style, but it's hard, not to say impossible, to be objective about your own leadership.

For all these reasons, even when the senior team does make time for diagnosis, frequently what emerges is what we call 'a laundry list' – a long, muddled list of symptoms and secondary causes that proves difficult to order or prioritise.

This is what happened with Aries. The problem with a laundry list is that it doesn't focus attention and resources where they are needed.

Benefits of a good diagnosis

A good diagnosis frames the situation. It drives the team to keep asking questions and changing perspectives until they get to root cause. It clears away the list of symptoms and secondary causes, focusing resources on what really needs attention.

The right diagnosis can radically transform the team's view of what they need to do. And because everyone on the team has had input throughout the process, they are galvanised and ready to put in the effort required to execute real change.

Coming to the right diagnosis can take time, but executing on the basis of a wrong diagnosis can be disastrous. Imagine if Peter had gone ahead and hired a new head of sales? And then, when nothing changed, hired or fired someone else? The board would be asking serious questions, and just imagine the impact on team morale!

Diagnosis

The diagnostic approach we recommend distils the laundry list down into the key issues really deserving of attention and resources.

Whilst we describe the diagnosis phase as a set of activities, do bear in mind that diagnosis is a continuous process. Think of it as something emergent. Your initial diagnosis should inform your thinking and dialogue as you work through The Growth Roadmap®. New awareness will emerge as you progress through each stage.

Diagnose across the business by working methodically through each of the four company areas – market, product, leadership and performance - asking *what will it take to win* in each area, and *what is the growth gap/opportunity*.

Use your learning to complete a succinct **Growth Diagnosis Statement** that summarises where the company has potential for growth and which challenges might get in the way. The Growth Diagnosis Statement puts the whole team on the same page.

Questions to Begin – Team Exercise

Before starting on the diagnosis we suggest completing this fun exercise, which can reveal some interesting insights about your company.

Ask two questions of the senior team:

- If this organisation were an animal, what animal would it be?

- If this organisation were a vehicle, what vehicle would it be?

The answers are often amusing, but also revealing. People who might be hesitant to admit their company was slow to react, complacent or risk averse are happy to describe it as being like an elephant, a hedgehog, or a tractor.

Don't assume you understand what each metaphor means – ask the person to describe briefly why they chose that particular animal or vehicle.

Gathering Data for the Diagnosis

Good diagnosis starts with accurate data. Winston Churchill had a famously overbearing leadership style but enough self-knowledge to know that if you have a strong personality, people tend to keep vital information from you. During World War II he created a separate Statistical Office whose job it was to give him continual, unfiltered facts about what was going on.

Gathering accurate data allows you to diagnose where the company is now. This in turn helps frame where you want to go and what it will take to get there. In order to complete the diagnosis worksheets that follow, you too will need to gather data. Here are some suggestions you may find useful.

Tips for Gathering Data

- Decide who in the organisation should contribute to the diagnosis. You may choose to include just the senior team or you may choose to broaden it out.

- Your mechanism for gathering data will in part be dictated by the number of people involved. If you have chosen to broaden out across the organisation, consider building a set of quantitative and qualitative questions into a survey. This allows you to collect lots of data efficiently.

- Detailed interviews with a structured question guide is a good way to gather data from a smaller group i.e. your senior team.

- If doing detailed interviews, the '5 Whys' (see Appendix 3) can be a useful tool to get under the hood of an issue raised.

- Good diagnosis is concrete, actionable and often quantitative. It frames issues in memorable words.

- Diagnosis may be helped by understanding the company's history and the founders' mindset, as well as social relationships across the board and the company.

- Give diagnosis the time it needs. Don't rush to diagnose – be curious. The obvious cause probably isn't the right one - dig deeper.

Four Company Areas: Market, Product, Leadership & Performance

For The Growth Roadmap®, we use four key areas when carrying out a business diagnosis: **Market**, **Product**, **Leadership** and **Performance**.

1. **Market**　2. **Product**　3. **Leadership**　4. **Performance**

After you've gathered data through targeted questions, surveys, face-to-face meetings and the '5 Why's' (see Appendix 3), complete a Growth Diagnostic Worksheet for each key area.

The Worksheets move through three sections:

- Where we are Now?

- What will it take to Win?

- What is the Growth Gap?

Where we are Now? involves distilling the data gathered into two or three priority issues for each key area.

What will it take to Win? draws on these issues to define what good would look like if these issues were addressed.

What is the Growth Gap? specifies the difference between 'what will it take to win' (expectations, ambition, opportunities, competitive advantage, strategic plans) and 'where we are now' (current performance, capability). It is the inherent tension between these two situations that gives rise to the choices and questions about what to change.

Growth Gap = [what will it take to win] – [where we are now]

Where possible the growth gap should be quantified and a timescale for resolution should be suggested. For example, the US is potentially our largest market, but growth there is flat. *If we hired a VP Sales US we could grow revenue by 20% year-on-year, within 24 months.*

Over the next few pages we will guide you through worksheets, which look at each of the four key areas – market, product, leadership and performance. We ask you to identify the gaps in each area.

1. Uncover Diagnosis – Market

When thinking about Market, consider size of market and whether the right people are focused on selling to the right sweet spot.

Seek to understand whether the team is focused on solving compelling customer problems and whether they have the skills to communicate the value they're delivering. Take into account competitors, new entrants and issues of regulatory, environmental and technological change, as well as political and economic developments.

Aries - Choosing the right market segment

Lumpy, long sales cycles and consistent reports from the sales team that the products were too expensive were just some of the challenges facing Aries Solutions, whose CEO Peter we met earlier.

During our initial survey and conversations with the sales team, it appeared that the product was just too expensive. But as we probed deeper, we discovered that Aries sold into a number of market segments and each had differing customer needs.

For customers in one segment – financial services – price wasn't an issue. They valued Aries' premium product and were willing to pay for it. But they found the product frustratingly difficult to implement; their priority was ease of use. In addition financial services was a bigger market opportunity.

In other market segments – telecoms and industrial waste – the customers also hankered after Aries' premium product but they didn't have the budget for it, so they constantly haggled on price and dragged sales cycles on forever. As one of the Aries sales team said, *"they have champagne taste but beer money"*.

It seemed Aries had two options: to bring the price down for customers with a lower budget, which would mean removing the product's premium attributes, or to find more customers with the resources to pay for quality.

Put like that, it was clear that Aries only had one option because lowering the standard of the product would mean ending up in a race to the bottom on price.

Before you complete your Market Worksheet here are some questions for you to reflect on.
There's no need to answer them all, but they should prompt some thinking.

Questions to consider on Market

Size of Market

- What size is the market and is it big enough to fulfil your growth ambitions?

- Are the markets you address growing or in decline?

- What is the growth rate of your key competitors?

- How can you compete profitably in these markets?

- What new markets should you enter and why?

- What were previous market entry plans? How did they work out?

Value Proposition & Sweet Spot

- How clear is the definition of your sweet spot?

- How focused is the sales team on selling to your sweet spot?

- How well do customers understand your proposition without face-to-face explanation?

- How compelling and urgent is the problem you solve?

- How would your customers rate your proposition when compared with the competition?

- Do you generate adequate new business leads?

- What new partners should you consider?

Stage 1. Uncover Diagnosis

Market Diagnosis Worksheet

Growth Diagnosis Worksheets are how we synthesise output from each diagnosis area. The first worksheet to complete is Market. Following discussions, data collation and root cause analysis complete your Market Diagnosis Worksheet.

Below is a worked example, and also space for you to explore your own growth gap. Keep the diagnosis priorities to two or three. Complete each row succinctly and ensure the growth gap is measurable and time-bound.

Aries Growth Diagnostic Worksheet – Market	Where we are Now?	What will it take to Win?	What is the Growth Gap?
	Financial services customers appreciate our premium product and are ready to pay for it but they seek much better ease of use.	Prioritise financial services and deliver a global proposition that allows us dominate that market. We need to invest in making our product easier to implement and training our sales team to sell into financial services.	Prioritising financial services could grow top line revenue by 25% per annum within 24 months and deliver better margins.

You have now completed the first worksheet of four. The others – product, leadership and performance, follow the same format. At the end of this stage you will draw them together into a Growth Diagnosis Statement.

2.  Uncover Diagnosis – Product

When thinking about Product, consider the external environment and the company's ability to beat the competition. Be curious about innovation and consider what technology changes are emerging and how well your products stack up against competitors.

Think about your existing way of doing business. Which areas need new processes to enable your business to scale more efficiently?

Aries - 'Build it and they will come'

Sweet spot customers in financial services loved Aries' product but were adamant that it had to be easier to implement.

Aries' CTO is a true expert in his field. He built the premium product to automate many of the challenges he himself had experienced. He was sure it did the job – his unspoken implication was that the financial services customers needed to catch up and had some learning to do.

As we probed deeper with the CTO and product designers, it became clear that their approach just didn't take the customer into account. Reviewing the product, we had to agree with the financial services customers: the screen design was clunky, implementation was difficult and customer support left a lot to be desired.

The root cause with Aries' product team appeared to be a deeply held belief that, as engineers, they knew best what the customer needed. They didn't feel an onus to speak with, or test their ideas with prospective customers, until very late in the process.

It was the CTO and engineers that had some learning to do. They needed to talk to target customers, adopt some good customer interviewing processes and deepen understanding. They needed to build products their customers actually wanted.

Stage 1. Uncover Diagnosis

Before you complete your Product Worksheet, here are some questions for you to reflect on. There's no need to answer them all, but they should prompt some thinking.

Questions to consider on Product

Scale

- How satisfied are international customers with your ability to deliver and support them?
- How could you make your product delivery more effective?
- How could you improve the process of getting new customers up and running? What impact would this have?
- What areas of your product are most in need of attention if you wish to scale?
- How partner ready are your products/services?

Innovation

- How good is your company at building and delivering new products and services?
- How well defined is your product roadmap?
- How does your product compare to the competition? Is it ahead? Or are you playing catch up?
- Do you ring-fence research and development (R&D) resources for new product development?

Differentiation

- How good are you at winning new customers?
- How much of a factor is price when you win or lose opportunities?
- How clear are you on protecting your difference?

Product Diagnosis Worksheet

Now following discussions, data collation and root cause analysis complete your Product Diagnosis Worksheet. Below is a worked example, and also space for you to explore your own growth gap. Keep your priorities to just two or three. Complete each row succinctly and make sure the growth gap is measurable and time-bound.

Aries Growth Diagnostic Worksheet – Product

Where we are Now?

Our priority customers are complaining that our product is too hard to implement and use.

What will it take to Win?

The customer-facing aspects of our product need to be dramatically improved. The product needs €1m–€2m further investment and at least 12 months before a new release will be ready. We need to add a strong product manager to become the 'voice of the customer' and enable us to scale.

What is the Growth Gap?

This new version could be transformative for our company. It could increase revenue by over 10% in the next 2 years.

3. Uncover Diagnosis – Leadership

For the CEO, CFO, Head of Sales and other leadership roles, this is a particularly challenging area. Self-diagnosis is really hard and may seem impossible. So get input here from the board, advisers and peers. Try to cultivate robust self-awareness and a very thick skin!

It is helpful to look at areas like clarity around shared vision, alignment of ambition and how the company is structured. Consider also leadership mindset, behaviours and capability.

Aries - Stepping out of the leader's shadow

Aries' CEO and co-founder, Peter, is talented, energetic and interested in everything. On any given day, he might be speaking with the Head of Telecoms in an Asian prospect and organising the office Christmas party.

The team really appreciate his commitment but after talking to them – both senior management and the layer below – it became clear that Peter has a problem delegating. He's a perfectionist who doesn't trust others to do the job as well as he can.

One team member made the interesting observation that Peter had a start-up mentality. *'He thinks he has to do everything. It's like he hasn't realised that the company has grown and evolved. He needs to adopt a scaling mindset.'*

At the same time, the CTO – the other co-founder – is an engineering whizz kid who had developed a tendency of always trusting his own judgment. His team, dazzled by his expertise, trusted him too. It had become all about what the CTO thought, and not about what the customer needed.

The decision to prioritise financial services entailed a company-wide refocus for Aries. Some on the senior team understood financial institutions better than Peter or the CTO. The time had come for the founders to learn to consult and make way for others. Their roles had to evolve in the same way the business had.

Before you complete your Leadership Worksheet, here are some questions for you to reflect on. There's no need to answer them all, but they should prompt some thinking.

Questions to consider on Leadership

Vision

- How aligned is the leadership team on direction?

- How well do employees understand the business objectives?

- How well equipped is the leadership team to implement change?

Capability

- What is the gap between what the leadership team says and what it actually does?

- How well does the leadership team prioritise key growth issues?

- How well does the organisational structure support your growth plans?

- What strengths or skills gaps are there in the team?

- How proficient are you at hiring good talent?

- Do team members hold each other accountable?

Mindset

- What is the existing senior leadership team mindset? How might it need to evolve?

- How much trust and respect is there within the team?

- How well does the senior leadership group perform as a team?

- How well is the leadership team supported and challenged by the board, external advisors or peer networks?

Leadership Diagnosis Worksheet

Now following discussions, data collation and root cause analysis, complete your Leadership Diagnosis Worksheet. Below is a worked example, and also space for you to explore your own growth gap. Keep priorities to just two or three. Complete each row succinctly and make sure the growth gap is measurable and time-bound.

Aries Growth Diagnostic Worksheet – Leadership

Where we are Now?	What will it take to Win?	What is the Growth Gap?
Talented CTO but tends to trust his own judgement, maybe too far. Team puts huge faith in him. Customer needs aren't being consulted.	A mindset shift in the CTO and engineering team – learn to be outward-looking and customer-focused and to take into account other perspectives.	We have an excellent market opportunity but to succeed we must embrace the 'voice of our chosen sweet spot'. This mindset shift and a product management focus are essential.

4. Uncover Diagnosis – Performance

In performance, we shine a light on shareholder expectations, and track record in meeting financial goals. We take a look at current levels of growth planning and how business assumptions are challenged.

Aries – Do the work on the numbers and bring the board with you

Peter had picked up on potential issues around sales velocity. As the diagnosis phase moved onto performance, it became clear that sales velocity in telecoms and industrial waste was worse than expected. Once we got the data, we realised that sales leads were at an all time low and losses against cheaper competitors were becoming more frequent. Encouragingly the market size for financial services looked more promising than originally thought.

All the signs were that price pressures would get worse and the sensitivity analysis did not look encouraging. Equally whilst financial services could bear much higher prices, the slow sales cycles meant cash would be tight. Additional funding would be needed.

Stage 1. Uncover Diagnosis

Before you complete your Performance Worksheet, here are some questions for you to reflect on. There's no need to answer them all, but they should prompt some thinking.

Questions to consider on Performance

Financial

- How reliable are your financial forecasts?
- How clear are employees on financial performance expectations?
- How well does the leadership team understand the financial model?
- How satisfied are shareholders with your growth rate?
- What impact would funding have on growth? How much funding would be required?
- How easy is it to access the funds needed to grow?

Internal Processes

- How is growth planning approached in the business?
- What are the key areas that need most attention?
- How robustly do you challenge your key business assumptions?
- What is your performance like compared to peers or best practice in your industry?
- What is the rhythm of measuring business performance?
- How clear are the metrics against which you measure progress?

Sales & Marketing

- How good are you at follow-on sales to existing customers?
- How reliable are your sales forecasts?
- What were expectations in previous years? How did you perform against these?
- What can you learn from this?

Performance Diagnosis Worksheet

Now following discussions, data collation and root cause analysis complete your Performance Diagnosis Worksheet. Below is a worked example, and also space for you to explore your own growth gap. Keep priorities to just two or three. Complete each row succinctly and make sure the growth gap is measurable and time-bound.

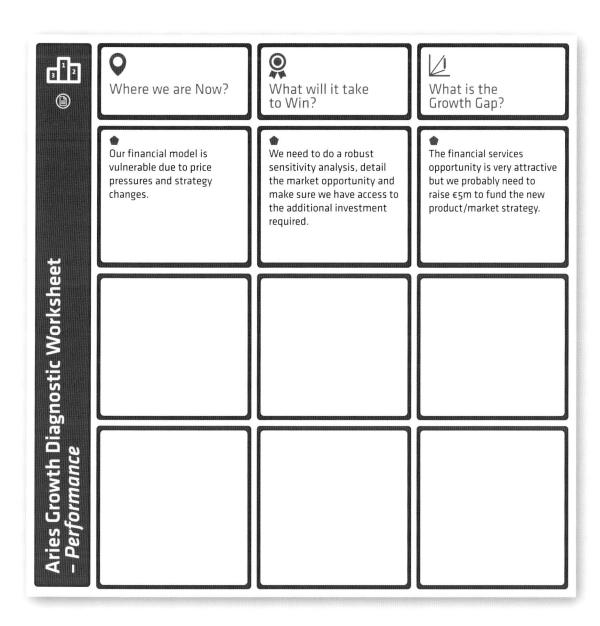

Aries Growth Diagnostic Worksheet – Performance

Where we are Now?	What will it take to Win?	What is the Growth Gap?
Our financial model is vulnerable due to price pressures and strategy changes.	We need to do a robust sensitivity analysis, detail the market opportunity and make sure we have access to the additional investment required.	The financial services opportunity is very attractive but we probably need to raise €5m to fund the new product/market strategy.

Stage 1. Uncover Diagnosis

Drawing your growth gap diagnosis together: *Growth Diagnosis Statement*

To complete the diagnosis phase, draw together the growth gap learnings onto one page. This enables each member of the team to grasp the key issues at a glance.

You now have a set of data from each of the four sections: market, product, leadership and performance. Consolidate this data into a clear set of emerging themes. This final stage of Diagnosis will help frame the key questions to be addressed as you work through The Growth Roadmap®.

 # Aries Growth Diagnosis Statement

Market

- Sales velocity is slowing in existing markets. If we focused more on the financial services sector, we could grow top line revenue by 25% within 2 years.

- We currently also provide solutions to telecoms and industrial waste. If we gradually withdraw from these market segments, it will improve our margins, as competition is cut throat.

Product

- Version 1 of our new product is too clunky and hard to use. We need to invest up to €2m to deliver Version 2 – this could increase revenue by 10% in 2 years.

- We must improve our product management function. We have premium financial services prospects who will pay well but we must deliver and exceed their expectation.

Leadership

- Our CEO needs to let go a bit, stop multi-tasking, and focus on the decisions that have critical business impact. Our CTO should consult more with customers regarding decisions around product.

- Our senior management team needs to step up and become a higher performing team with clearer accountability.

Performance

- The market opportunity in financial services is much bigger than we previously thought. We believe we can compete and win here successfully.

- We need to raise €5m to fund the new strategy and product investment. Initial discussions with our investors suggest that they would be prepared to back a proposed aggressive growth plan.

We provide a blank Growth Diagnosis Statement in the Worksheets section at the back of this book, so you can complete your own company diagnosis.

"Good business leaders create a vision, articulate the vision, passionately own the vision, and relentlessly drive it to completion".

JACK WELCH

 Stage 2. Commit to a Shared Vision

Aquarius

Aquarius is a
technology company
providing micro
heart pacemakers
to improve quality
of life.

Aquarius is a client of ours providing micro heart pacemakers. With a disruptive business model and market-leading technology that targets improved quality of life, they had achieved significant success since start-up, dominating their local market.

But growth was beginning to stall and the team was becoming frustrated. Working through Stage 1 Uncover Diagnosis yielded a surprising finding: the leadership team didn't seem clear and aligned about what direction to go in or what goals to set. Some of the newer senior team members had significant international experience and were more gung-ho about scaling into global markets than the founders, but they weren't being included in decision-making.

Our research had pinpointed a huge emerging opportunity for micro pacemakers. Aquarius appeared to have the capability but they hadn't put a strategy in place to capitalise on the opportunity and were struggling to scale the business. We felt that they would benefit from working on their Shared Vision. The Co-Founder CEO, Laura, didn't dispute the diagnosis but she was surprised.

"We had such a strong purpose launching this company," she told us. *"We wanted to provide better quality of life for patients with heart conditions. The father of one of our founders suffered with a pacemaker he found uncomfortable. We felt there must be a better way. The whole team connected with this. From our point of view, we already have a great vision".*

She was right that Aquarius did indeed have a strong founding purpose, one which really resonated with people. But shared vision goes well beyond the founders' purpose – it's about setting goals to drive ambition, developing the right mindset for success and ensuring that purpose remains inspirational and relevant.

Shared vision isn't something static, it evolves as the company evolves. Markets, products and industries are changing all the time, and vision changes with them. The right mindset for start-up may not be the right mindset for scale.

The frustration felt by Aquarius' new international team members indicated that the original purpose of the founders was becoming diluted, and was no longer enough to align the team. Add to this the increased complexity of operating in new global markets, with new investors, and it was clear – Aquarius needed a new, restated vision that would drive transformation.

Shared Vision is important

Successful companies have a shared vision of the direction they are taking. Put simply, in the words of business strategist, Peter Senge, a shared vision is a *"force in people's hearts, a force of compelling power.... a deep purpose that expresses the organisation's reason for existence".*

Look back at the Jack Welch quote we chose for this chapter. He emphasises that vision not only has to be created and articulated, it also has to be *'relentlessly driven to completion'.* Shared vision isn't just a logo or slogan that's embedded in your company's masthead and never revised – vision needs to be actioned, like everything else.

In the absence of a shared vision, employees tend to pursue their own, short-term goals. This is natural. Some team members may be more ambitious than others. Some may wish to build an international world-beating product, others may be keener on building deep relationships with a select few customers closer to home.

Lack of a shared vision causes team members to pull in different directions and to set different priorities. The result is predictable – pettiness, slower than anticipated progress and ultimately chaos. Your shared vision should have the power to inspire your team in the interests of a common purpose.

A compelling founding purpose is important. But if our experience has taught us anything it's that companies that seek to scale need to periodically review and transform their vision and purpose.

It's also useful to consider the perspective of your board, investors and stakeholders. They are invested in your success. Getting commitment to a compelling vision and being clear about where you are headed provides direction and motivation for everyone involved.

Change won't happen unless leadership teams challenge themselves hard on vision, with questions like:

- Do we have a common purpose? Is the team still aligned around it? Is this purpose still inspirational and relevant in today's world?

- Is the team challenging itself with ambitious goals?

- Does the leadership mindset need to shift?

- What does success look like? What are we going to be famous for?

The Growth Roadmap® – Definition of Shared Vision

In The Growth Roadmap®, we have a particular understanding of shared vision. Our definition focuses on transformation and closing the growth gap – building tension between where the business is today and what the future looks like.

We'd add one extra phrase to Welch's great quote: *"Good business leaders create a vision, articulate the vision, passionately own the vision, relentlessly drive it to completion"...* **"and then they repurpose their vision for the next stage of transformation".**

Our definition of shared vision incorporates company purpose, stretch goals and mindset and we suggest that it's reviewed every three or four years.

We also put dates and figures on vision, not invariably, but where appropriate. Your company purpose should be inspirational but your stretch goals should be targeted. Inspiration without targets doesn't drive action.

A strong shared vision makes every member of your team feel part of a bigger purpose. It gives them a sense of mission, pride and ownership. It inspires them to raise their ambition. It shifts the mindset from seeing obstacles to spotting opportunities. It changes the mantra from *'that's impossible'* to *'how would we do that?'*

Try to articulate your vision succinctly. Make it memorable so that it can serve as a linchpin for your team. Some visions are passionate rallying cries, others are practical and down-to-earth. All must be easily visualised. Yours should be unique and reflect your strengths. It will probably take more than one sitting to craft, and it's best not to force it.

In the Kennedy era, someone asked the guy sweeping the floor at the space agency NASA what he was doing. He replied *"I'm helping to put a man on the moon".* That, to us, is a perfect shared vision: it's succinct and inspirational; it's owned by the whole team, from the astronauts to the cleaners; it includes an ambitious but achievable goal which incorporates *'how will this be done?'*

And, finally, this vision isn't fixed, it looks ahead to the next phase of transformation – once the man is on the moon? Time to set a new vision: Mars.

Cover Story Exercise

When working with your team to start exploring shared vision, it's a good idea to loosen up thinking to get people out of the day-to-day. This Cover Story Exercise is designed to do just that.

Your team become journalists who are tasked with writing news articles describing what your company will look like in a few years. This is enjoyable but more importantly, significant themes emerge from this exercise.

- Form small groups - set aside an hour or two to act as journalists.

- Agree a date in the future – select a real publication you could imagine yourself or your company being featured in.

- Ask each group to write a 300 word article describing what your industry will look like and what your company will have achieved.

 Some Tips

- Start with a catchy headline that will grab the reader's attention.

- State the main achievement up-front and then fill in the background of how it happened. Use quotes, statistics, metaphors and images to bring the story to life.

- Get the group to stretch their imaginations – don't let them be constrained by practical concerns or by wondering how their ambition might be realised.

- The exercise should be fun and engaging, it should take people out of their day-to-day concerns and start to create a sense of energy and commitment to a compelling future.

Where the cover stories go

The 'stories' that team members write are presented at your first shared vision session. During that session draw out the themes, ideas and ambitions that can contribute to the shared vision.

- Capture the similarities and differences in the various cover stories.
  - Explore the themes that arise – the common ones and the more imaginative or 'off-trend' stories that emerge.
  - Have team members converged on their stories?
  - Are some people more focused on customer satisfaction or revenue?
  - Are some stories more ambitious?

All these questions will provide material for your shared vision discussion.

The Growth Roadmap® approach to crafting a shared vision has three interconnected parts:

1.   **Defining your Company Purpose**

What's our cause? Why is this important? What impact will we have? Why should anyone care? What is our personal why?

2.   **Setting Stretch Goals**

What will our company look like in three years? What might success be? What goals should we set for performance?

3.   **Shifting the Leadership Team Mindset**

How do we do things around here? What mindset guides behaviour in our senior leadership team? Are these thinking patterns still helpful? Will they serve us well or do they need to be tweaked?

1. Commit to a Shared Vision: Defining your Company Purpose

Purpose matters. It's the 'Why' we do what we do. Talented people have choices. Purpose can provide a cause, a reason to belong for your team. The purpose may be local or global – it could be inventing a new medicine or technology that makes life easier.

At the beginning of this chapter we introduced the founders of Aquarius who launched with a truly inspiring purpose. They wanted to ensure good quality of life for people with pacemakers. They had a personal story around this, involving the father of one of the founders. Their passion was communicated to shareholders, investors and to every new company hire.

But as the business grew, the purpose became diluted. They were being challenged by competitors who were also focusing on quality of life. To show that they were the best company to deliver micro pacemakers in global markets, they reset their purpose to include a focus on innovation.

Scorpio

Scorpio is a technology company with a financial platform that manages funding for investors and enables small companies to apply for loans.

By contrast another client of ours, Scorpio, felt this 'purpose stuff' was empty rhetoric and platitude. Their CEO complained that employees weren't fully engaged or delivering on their potential. She couldn't understand why. People were well paid, benefits were good and the bonus scheme stood to make many of the team rich. She felt this was all the purpose they needed.

Scorpio had a financial platform which managed funding for investors and enabled growing companies to apply for loans. In our work with Scorpio, we reached beyond the senior team and selected a group of employees to work with and craft the company purpose statement.

This 'bottom up' approach to drawing out the company's purpose worked well. After sharing their personal purpose and some stories about the company, the team created and worked on some initial drafts. Here's what they came up with:

"In Scorpio, we believe that economic growth in communities matters. We are building a technology platform to enable small companies to access loans that help them grow and employ more people".

This purpose statement struck an emotional chord with many in the business. The CFO started to see that people might care about this purpose as much as their pay and benefits. The CEO and the rest of the leadership team started to communicate this purpose relentlessly. They talked about it during interviews to check if candidates were a good fit. They told stories about the impact they made – demonstrating that their purpose statement was more than a slogan.

The purpose statement gave meaning to the development team working on the platform. It engaged the sales team. It influenced business direction and decision-making. Employee promoter scores went up. And of course, good economic results followed.

Without a clear purpose, performance can only ever be sub-optimal. Research by Malnight et al*, published in Harvard Business Review, highlights just how important purpose is. They launched a study of global growth companies to investigate the strategies driving their growth. What they uncovered was that many of these growth companies had used purpose as a lever for growth. Moving purpose from the periphery of their strategy to its core, they had used it to generate sustained profitable growth, stay relevant in a rapidly changing world and deepen their ties with stakeholders.

Your purpose statement should be simple, clear and actionable. It should strike an emotional chord and enable your team to derive meaning from what they do. Here are some questions to discuss to help derive your purpose:

Questions to consider on Purpose Statement

- Why did you join the company?

- What is your company's founding story?

- What inspires you to come to work each day?

- What is your cause?

- Why do we exist (beyond financial gain)?

- When did you feel most proud to work for the company?

- Why did you feel proud?

- What specific contributions has your company made to the lives of others?

- What has been the impact of those contributions?

*Put Purpose at the Core of Your Strategy by Thomas W Malnight, Ivy Buche and Charles Dhanarja, Harvard Business Review, 2019

Company Purpose Worksheet

Discuss and debate questions like those above and complete your own Company Purpose Worksheet. Try to keep it both brief and meaningful. We share some ideas and a space for you to work through your own company purpose.

We suggest a structure similar to the format below.

To *(insert the **contribution**)*, so that *(insert the **impact**)*.

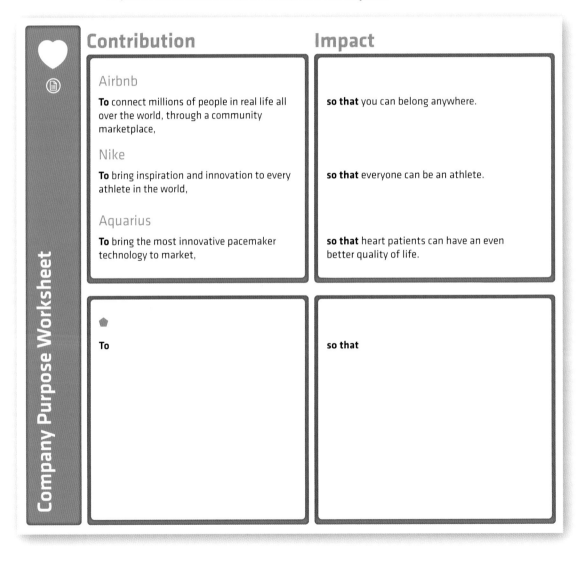

Company Purpose Worksheet

Contribution

Airbnb

To connect millions of people in real life all over the world, through a community marketplace,

Nike

To bring inspiration and innovation to every athlete in the world,

Aquarius

To bring the most innovative pacemaker technology to market,

To

Impact

so that you can belong anywhere.

so that everyone can be an athlete.

so that heart patients can have an even better quality of life.

so that

2. Commit to a Shared Vision: Setting Stretch Goals

Your Cover Story exercise will have filled the room with ambitious, inspiring shared vision themes. The Purpose exercise will have clarified what your company stands for. That's the fun bit! Now it's time to support your purpose with specific three year stretch goals.

A great founding purpose gives 'lift off' to the company but if you want to find new markets and develop new products, you need to set goals.

Setting stretch goals was the beginning of truly transformative change for Aquarius. At this stage, they had decent revenue of €23 million per annum. The diagnostic phase had revealed that there were really strong opportunities for their micro pacemaker and they would have the advantage of getting in early. Based on this, they set a revenue goal of €100 million in three years time.

The ambition of the Aquarius team went beyond incremental growth. They wanted to scale the business internationally. But it wasn't an absolutely impossible goal – it was grounded in reality, after a close analysis of the global pacemaker market.

Laura, the CEO, later admitted to us that she didn't actually expect to meet the €100 million target in three years. But she hoped ambition would bring momentum to the team. She was right. After 24 months they had improved the technology, made two acquisitions and strengthened the team. Yes, there were a myriad of challenges along the way, and a few casualties to address – but they were on track to meet their stretch goal.

Aquarius is a good role model. When it comes to setting your own stretch goals, establish clear definitions of 'what success looks like' and put in place timetables for achievement. Draw on the work you did in the diagnostic phase to understand your own particular growth gaps. Take inspiration from the cover story exercise, and the discussions afterwards.

Seek to agree a limited number of stretch goals. Setting a stretch goal in each of the four key business areas works well – market, product, leadership and performance. The goals are interdependent and impact each other. For instance, once Aquarius had set their revenue goal, they needed to address team capability and new sales targets.

Questions to consider when Setting Stretch Goals

 Market

- What are industry experts saying about market direction?
- How many customers will you have?
- What value will you offer them?
- Which competitors will you defeat?

 Product

- What products will you offer?
- What value propositions?
- What new services?
- What new competencies will you be developing?

 Leadership

- What will your leadership capability be?
- How many staff and what kind of skills will they have?
- What culture will you aspire to?
- How will it be regarded externally?

 Performance

- How will you look to your shareholders?
- What will your revenue be?
- What will your profit be?
- What will your growth rate be?

Tips on Setting Stretch Goals

- Think about beating a particular competitor by a certain date – through market share, revenue or some other measurable goal.

- Emulating a particular company may help if you have role models in mind – 'be the next...'

- After reflecting on draft stretch goals, think about how you might select one of these as a unifying stretch goal or north star that is easy to communicate – for example, a stretch goal 'to be recognised by Gartner (a leading analyst firm) as the global leader in payments security', is more concrete than the goal 'to be recognised as a global payment security company'.

Company Stretch Goals Worksheet

Following debate and discussion use the reflection questions on the previous page to start documenting your stretch goals in the worksheet. Use the Aquarius sample below to guide you on format and approach. Keep stretch goals to just two or three in each company area. Make sure each stretch goal is measurable and time-bound.

Aquarius' Stretch Goals Worksheet

 ### Market

- Deliver 50% year-on-year growth in sales
- Build a world class sales team
- 6,000 customers worldwide by X date

 ### Product

- Reduce pacemaker size by 35% to create a micro pacemaker
- Increase pacemaker battery life by 40%
- Wifi enable to support emergency communications

 ### Leadership

- Become recognised as the company that top medtech graduates want to work with by X date
- Challenge ourselves to become a higher performing team

 ### Performance

- Achieve €100m revenue by X date
- Achieve EBITDA of 15% by X date

3.  Commit to a Shared Vision: Shifting the Leadership Team Mindset

Scaling a business invariably involves change. Working through Purpose and Stretch Goals sets out the future direction. This both challenges and aligns the team. But change ultimately involves a shift in the leadership team's mindset.

The leadership team's mindset is the collection of attitudes, beliefs, assumptions and behaviours that steer the company. Mindset determines how the leadership team prioritises, makes decisions and what behaviours it rewards.

Mindset can be tricky to get a hold of. You won't see it written down in a financial report. It's not normally part of a strategic plan. Yet it lies beneath the surface of everything you do – a bit like the proverbial iceberg.

Mindset is what has got your company to where it is today. But mindset shouldn't be carved in stone.

As your company evolves, grows and responds to different opportunities, so too should the leadership mindset. There are parts of mindset that you will never want to change. But there may be others that are no longer serving you well, and these need to change.

Scaling may require finding a different approach to what has worked previously. Continual learning and innovation are key. A 'fixed mindset' isn't open or adaptive to change – what you want is a 'growth mindset'.

Leadership teams that close the growth gap challenge themselves on mindset. What needs to stay and what is no longer serving the business well? This is particularly important for firms led by founder-entrepreneurs who may identify fixedly with their founding vision.

We position mindset as step three of shared vision but in practice companies generally work on stretch goals and mindset in tandem: a shift in mindset enables a more creative and radical approach to setting goals, but equally an ambitious goal can provide the momentum needed to progress mindset.

The mindset shift for Aquarius began during the setting of the stretch goals. The more the team debated, the more their ambition became clear. Setting a stretch revenue goal of €100m was unnerving for many, but it was remarkable how the mindset of the whole team shifted as they focused on scaling up and delivering the new goal.

They began to think like the global business they needed to be if they were to scale. For us, it was inspiring to see the mindset shift in even the most conservative team member from *'We're fine as we are'* to *'What would meeting our target look like? How would we do it? What would we need to change?'*

When a team starts asking 'How?' rather than erecting barriers, they have started to shift to a growth mindset. Just as different companies have different mindsets, which depend on their history, personnel and the industry they operate in, the reasons they might need to adapt their mindset can also be different.

For instance, a company that began life with a strong sales mindset driven by the entrepreneurial spirit of its founding team may need to adjust to a more market focused approach as it grows globally. A mindset that is too sales-oriented ('all sales are good') might have difficulty adjusting to a more market led and disciplined approach.

Questions to consider on Leadership Team Mindset

Leadership team members behave the way they do because of what they think (mindset) and believe (values). For the most part, these are invisible. Documenting and sharing them helps clarify the current mindset and starts a conversation about what might need to change.

When reflecting on the mindset of your current leadership team, consider the following questions:

- What are the key **characteristics** of our mindset today? Entrepreneurial, family, results oriented, process oriented, risk takers, risk averse, political, aggressive, ambitious?

- What is **important** in this team? What are key strengths in our existing mindset?

- What gets **rewarded**? What do we value – speed, reflection, fairness? What does the team talk/not talk about? How flexible or process oriented are we?

- What are key **personal values**? Trust, loyalty, friendship, commitment to innovation, challenge, respect, status, teamwork, personal development, openness, integrity?

- What are **key performance indicators (KPIs)**? Winning in marketplace, sales, revenue, profit, development of people, staff retention?

A final tip: Make sure to document and note the mindset elements you wish to keep and never want to see change!

Once you have discussed, debated and defined the leadership team mindset today, use a similar set of questions to determine what the leadership team mindset needs to evolve to.

Leadership Team Mindset Worksheet

Once you have reflected on the leadership questions suggested and completed your discussions, document the results in the Leadership Team Mindset Worksheet. Use the Aquarius example to guide you on a format and approach. Below we have left some space for you to document your own thoughts on how leadership team mindset might need to evolve. Again, keep it succinct and focus on a limited few proposed mindset shifts.

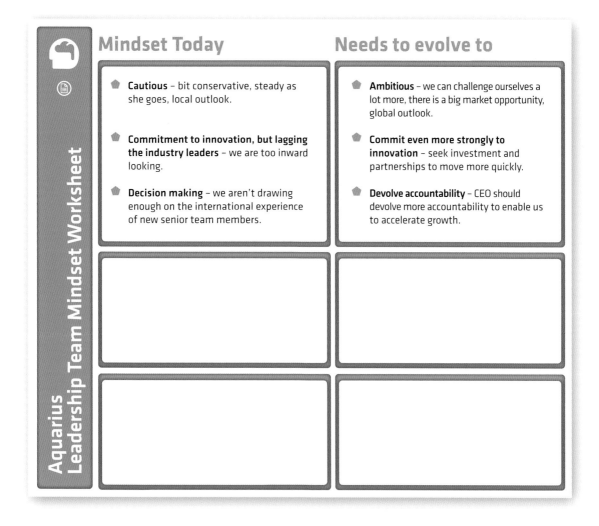

Aquarius Leadership Team Mindset Worksheet

Mindset Today	Needs to evolve to
Cautious – bit conservative, steady as she goes, local outlook.	**Ambitious** – we can challenge ourselves a lot more, there is a big market opportunity, global outlook.
Commitment to innovation, but lagging the industry leaders – we are too inward looking.	**Commit even more strongly to innovation** – seek investment and partnerships to move more quickly.
Decision making – we aren't drawing enough on the international experience of new senior team members.	**Devolve accountability** – CEO should devolve more accountability to enable us to accelerate growth.

And finally, your Shared Vision Statement

The final step is to draw on the learning from the exercises in this chapter to craft your Shared Vision Statement.

Take your time. It will probably take more than one sitting to craft and refine it. Don't force it. We find that drafting a version and then taking time to *sit with it* can be a helpful process to follow.

Our guidance is that your Shared Vision Statement should focus on a timeframe of three years. This creates the right balance and tension between stretching the team, but also emphasising the need to start executing to deliver now.

Tips on writing a Shared Vision Statement

- **Try opening with phrases like:**
  Be like *(insert name of company you admire)*
  Be recognised by the market as the company that....

- **Use analogies or metaphors:**
  Be the Amazon of pharmaceutical products
  Be the Honda 50 of solar-powered motorbikes

- **Follow your Mindset:**
  As a senior leadership team, dig deep into your own mindset and beliefs to ensure you are clear about why your shared vision matters to you. For others to follow, they need to trust you. Real communication is distinguished by its honesty – if they feel you are faking it, you will never make it.

- **Be prepared for, and welcome, resistance:**
  It's better to have creative conflict and debate than a sham consensus that nobody believes in. Your shared vision statement should motivate and inspire your team to take small steps, no matter how hesitant.

- **Don't be afraid to revisit:**
  By this stage your shared vision statement is in draft. Hold it in the back of your mind as you work through the rest of the roadmap. Check-in as you go through to see if your shared vision statement needs to be tweaked.

- Remember this shared vision statement is for internal communication to your team. It is not intended for external use.

Shared Vision Statement

You have now completed exercises on purpose, stretch goals and mindset. You have documented the outputs into the relevant worksheets. Now pull together these drafts into a single Shared Vision Statement. The Aquarius example below and the tips provided should guide format and approach.

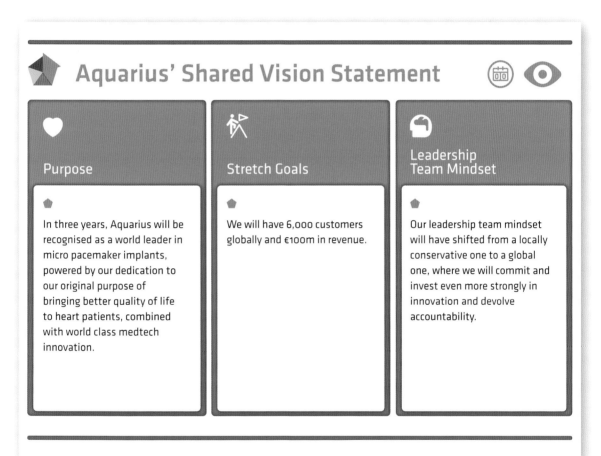

We include a blank Shared Vision Statement in the Worksheets section for you to complete your own.

"Companies rarely die from moving too fast and they frequently die from moving too slow".

REID HASTINGS,
FOUNDER CEO NETFLIX

Stage 3. Select the Right Strategy

If shared vision encapsulates the purpose, goals and direction of your company, your Strategy describes how you are going to get there. Where shared vision is inspiring, motivating and aspirational; strategy is concrete, grounded and specific. Think of it as the steps to operationalise your vision. No company can succeed without a clear strategy. This is something we've learnt the hard way, both as entrepreneurs and as advisors to other businesses.

Gemini

Gemini is a technology company that deliver banking software to large international banks.

Let's meet Gemini, a business we were involved with a number of years ago. They delivered banking software to international banks. The founders saw themselves as a product company and had a clear vision to build a software product that could be delivered to banks globally.

Gemini started out by reeling in a few big customers: major international banks, willing to pay well for their expertise. It was an exciting start, but after a few years, there was palpable frustration and tension in the company. Gemini's customers didn't want a product 'out of the box' – they wanted customised software. These were large banks with the resources to put behind these projects, determined to tweak the software exactly the way they wanted it.

This meant a lot of service and hand-holding. Gemini's best people were constantly tied up with customers. It was time-consuming and people-heavy. The revenue was large but profit was poor. The engineering team was frustrated, they wanted to build a product but couldn't. Shareholders were becoming increasingly angsty because they weren't interested in investing in a profit-poor company.

The leadership team was torn between their aspiration to build a world beating product and the reality of ongoing customer bespoke services. The team had ambitions to scale, but had stagnated and were being held back by their existing customers. The revenue from these bespoke services was keeping the company alive, but lack of focus on product meant the dream of building a global software company remained just that, a dream.

Gemini was failing to deliver on its shared vision. They had made a classic mistake: excited by a few big customers, they were dancing to their customers' tune and this was taking them further and further away from their core vision. They lacked deep understanding of the investment, disciplines and skills needed to realise their vision. In short, they hadn't strategised their vision.

Most CEOs will tell you that they know how important it is to have a strategy. Many will assure you that they do actually have one. But probe a bit and, typically, you'll discover that the strategy is vague or exists only in the CEO's head. Often it's not articulated clearly to the team; sometimes it's a few words on a slide.

A good strategy is worked through with the whole team in a rigorous process. It is tested, reviewed regularly and updated when necessary. It links up decision-making with follow-through actions. It reflects the perspective of the entire team – even the most brilliant CEO can't strategise alone. Most importantly, it is contextualised and documented. If it isn't written down, it isn't a strategy – it's a collection of ideas.

Why Strategy is hard

Why is this so hard to achieve? Well, Gemini's story is instructive. Particularly when starting out, it's natural to go 'where the money is', without considering whether this is the direction you want to go in, or whether revenue will yield profit. And of course, this approach is inherently unscalable. Before you know it, the team is overwhelmed by the day-to-day and it seems like there is no time to reset.

The lack of clarity around the definition of the term strategy doesn't help. It's such a broad, generic term, used in so many situations, it can be difficult to be concrete about what it means. If you haven't defined what strategy is in *your* context, then how can you and your team create and implement one?

The Growth Roadmap® Definition of Strategy

In The Growth Roadmap® we define strategy as the set of steps you take to operationalise your shared vision. Strategy is a set of choices that fit coherently together and provide a clear direction. These choices should clearly state what your company is going to do and equally what it is not going to do. These choices need to be clear and actionable for the team. We take each 'strategic step' in 12 month chunks.

Strategy in The Growth Roadmap® context answers the question, *"How will we achieve our shared vision given our diagnosis of the terrain?"* In mountaineering terms, your strategy stakes out the best route to the top of the mountain, based on the company's capabilities and where you are starting from.

Strategy should be a continuous process. It's not something you do once a year and shelve for the following 12 months. Strategy is a way of thinking – the team gets aligned around a targeted approach, which is then reviewed and updated regularly. In this way, strategy becomes part of the fabric of your company.

The benefits of a good Strategy

A good strategy makes direction clear to each company area – marketing, sales, product, human resources etc. It gets everybody on the same page, removing ambiguity.

A good strategy means the same thing to every member of your team and to every audience you explain it to, on every occasion.

In The Growth Roadmap®, we've devised a set of steps to help you build a strategy and embed it. This process delivers a bold strategy statement, which helps everyone make the right choices, take the right actions and evaluate progress against shared vision.

Dual Track – Exploit and Explore

Before we turn to building your strategy statement, let's take a look at the tension, or dual track, that exists in most businesses.

Most canny leadership teams recognise that they should be scanning two horizons: both existing and potential opportunities. It can feel like the team is being pulled in two different directions but the truth is it's important to be pursuing dual tracks. A team that is exploiting and exploring its horizons is actually pursuing dual tracks in parallel. All successful companies do this - and they keep on doing it because today's emerging opportunity is tomorrow's new one.

The Growth Roadmap® goes beyond the conventional approach of conceiving a single strategy for the business. We call our approach the Dual Track. Scaling depends on doing both – it's never either/or! Teams that transform growth are like the Roman god Janus, who had two faces: one looking to the present and the other to the future.

How Netflix leveraged the dual track approach

Household name Netflix are masters of the dual track approach. They began in the late 1990s as an online DVD rental store based on monthly subscriptions – that was their existing market and they exploited it to the hilt. But to truly scale and deliver on their ambitions they needed to do more. From 2005 they were exploring, in parallel, the new market of online streaming. They invested in technology to improve this and by 2008 the streaming market had moved from explore to exploit and they were on to the next exploratory market: creating their own content. They invested in their first original series, House of Cards, which debuted in 2013. The market for original content is currently a long way from saturation.

If Netflix hadn't pursued the dual track from the start, constantly balancing exploit and explore, they couldn't have achieved their astonishing disruption of such an established creative industry nor scaled the business the way they have. By pursuing the dual track, they evolved from a video rental company to taking on Hollywood studios.

This approach doesn't just apply to unicorns like Netflix. In Gemini's case, their frustration came from their lack of clarity around exploit and explore, their tendency to mix all their markets in together and not draw a clear line between their existing customers – large banks – and potential new customers who might prove a better fit. Once they grasped the dual track, they had the beginnings of a strategy.

The world doesn't stand still while your team is strategising, and neither should you. Plan for the short term in a deliberate way and take a disciplined approach to experimenting with new products/markets.

Recognising your Dual Tracks

Caught in the day-to-day? It can be challenging to differentiate between exploit and explore. Here are some guidelines to help:

Dual Track Process

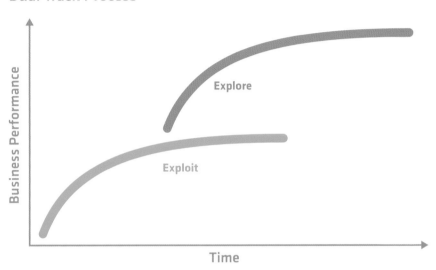

Track 1: Exploit

Your existing 'exploit' market is where the bulk of your business/revenue is today. The majority of the company's resources, both people and funding, may be tied up here, typically about 80%. Your business has achieved product/market fit and this stage is about exploiting that.

To gain insight into your exploit market, discuss these questions with your team:

1. How can we improve performance in our core business?

2. What incremental innovations can we achieve in the core to improve growth?

3. How can we up-sell or cross-sell more to existing customers?

Track 2: Explore

Your 'explore' track typically involves getting into a new market, testing a new product concept or finding a new application for existing technology. Perhaps a new business model, pricing, partners or digitisation. The mantra here is entrepreneurial. The structure should be flexible enough to cope with a changing environment. There is a high level of uncertainty. It's a learning process. Try things out, run quick experiments, act in order to think. Typically, about 20% of company resources should be allocated to explore.

The focus for exploit differs significantly from the focus for explore and running the two in parallel can be tricky. In exploit companies are executing a strategy, whilst in explore, just like a start-up, your company is looking to find a new strategy or business model, perhaps with new customers, products or ways of doing business.

The focus in exploit is on management and process, failure is not okay. In explore the focus is on entrepreneurial intuition and it can feel unstructured and messy. Testing and small failures should be viewed as learning opportunities. Running a dual track of exploit and explore means there can be tension between them.

To keep the team aligned and clear it can be helpful to understand the drivers behind each track and how they differ.

Exploit and Explore – *the key characteristics of each track*

Focus	Exploit	Explore
🧺 **Market**	● Service existing customers better ● Incremental innovation	● High degree of uncertainty ● Validate customer problems – possible disruptive innovation
📦 **Product**	● Product/Market fit achieved ● Product management disciplines strong ● Organised planning	● Build prototypes or minimum viable products ● Improve iteratively
🏃 **Leadership**	● Manage and improve today's performance ● Make decisions based on sound data ● Hierarchical organisational structure	● Entrepreneurial insights and disciplined hypothesis testing ● Act fast based on limited data ● Small, nimble squads or possibly just CEO learning and iterating
📊 **Performance**	● Financial metrics – revenue, profit etc ● Exception reporting	● Borrow from lean startup principles ● Data from customer experiments, customer experience, uptake in pilots, retention, transition to paying customer ● Failure part of learning process

Building your Strategy Statement

Now that you have an understanding of the dual track and are starting to think about which markets to exploit and which to explore, let's take this with us to the next stage, and build your one-page strategy statement.

We've divided this process into four steps:

1.  **Gaining Industry Insight**
   Seek insight into your industry and sector. Look at upcoming trends, technologies and customers needs. How is your industry changing? Can you diagnose unarticulated customer needs? How can you meet those needs?

2. **Setting Strategic Objectives**
   What primary objective will you set to drive the strategy? Will you focus on revenue, profit or market share?

3. **Clarifying Product/Market Scope**
   This clarifies which customers you will go after, and with what products/services. Who are your sweet spot customers and what value are you offering them, compared to the competition? Can you measure that value?

4. **Creating Competitive Advantage**
   A good test of your strategy is to consider what advantage you have over the competition. Here we look at understanding your competitive advantage across the criteria that matter most to your customers.

1. Select the Right Strategy: Gaining Industry Insight

Strategy starts with gaining insight into your industry and how it is changing. Insight should pre-empt trends – it's about spotting gaps in the market and/or product applications and understanding unarticulated customer need before your competitors do.

Some individuals have uncanny insight. They instinctively know where they have to be next, like the great Canadian ice hockey player, Wayne Gretzky, who said "*I skate to where the puck is going to be, not to where it has been*". Or like Steve Jobs who seemed to intuit what people wanted from technology before they knew it themselves.

We can't all be born a Gretzky or Jobs. And we don't have to be. You can learn to develop insight. In our experience, what distinguishes insightful people is their curiosity and their focus. They're always asking questions and gathering data. They're good at listening and if they're not happy with the first answer, they keep on asking. As a result, they always seem to know what's happening before anyone else does. They're also flexible, adaptive and creative – much more likely to say 'why not' and 'what if', than 'no'.

The good news is that scaling companies have a great advantage when it comes to seeking insight. They are nimble and they're closer to their customers than their bigger rivals.

To gain insight, reflect again on the work you did in Uncover Diagnosis, the first stage of The Growth Roadmap®. What have you learnt about your industry and related industries? Use tools like the '5 Why's' (Appendix 3) to understand your customers and to diagnose their needs. Stay open-minded. Consider 'what if' your customers' problems could be solved in a different way.

After gathering data from customers, brainstorm with your team. Consider questions like the following:

> * What are the shared beliefs in our industry?
> * What emerging trends could change these beliefs?
> * What regulatory issues could change the game?
> * Where are the big players or startups investing?
> * What can we learn from how other industries have developed?

Questions to consider on Industry Insight

Insight is deeply personal. It blends both intuition and creativity. It can be an exciting 'Eureka' or 'lightbulb' moment that comes out of analysis of hard data, deep knowledge of your industry and a synthesis of what your team has learnt.

Gemini: Industry Insight

Understanding the dual track brought Gemini insight. They realised first, that delivering customised software was unscalable and was never going to return a decent profit, since revenue was being eaten up by customer service. **If we want to scale and create shareholder value, we have to build product** – was their first insight.

Their second insight came from talking to other players in their industry. They discovered that mid-sized banks didn't have the large IT departments required to manage customised services. These banks were often controlled by business people who operated differently to large banks and preferred a cloud-based product that would work 'out of the box' without lengthy implementation cycles. Gemini's second insight sounds simple but it changed everything: **Mid-sized banks are a better fit for us than our existing large banking customers**.

Inherent to this insight was the assumption that they had the capabilities and knowledge to build a shrink-wrapped product for mid-sized banks. This assumption was something they would need to rigorously test as they began to explore this market.

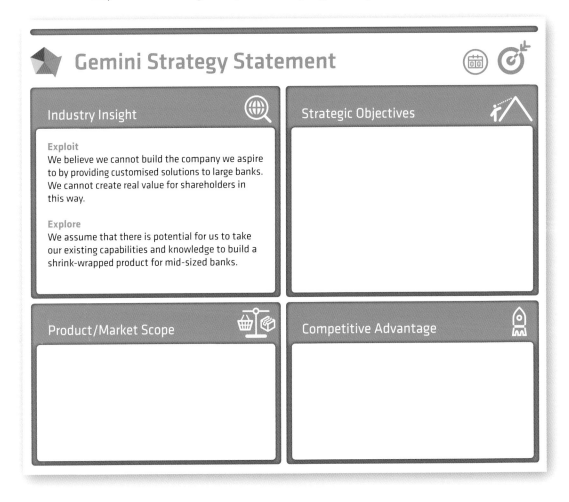

Gemini Strategy Statement

Industry Insight

Exploit
We believe we cannot build the company we aspire to by providing customised solutions to large banks. We cannot create real value for shareholders in this way.

Explore
We assume that there is potential for us to take our existing capabilities and knowledge to build a shrink-wrapped product for mid-sized banks.

Strategic Objectives

Product/Market Scope

Competitive Advantage

2. Select the Right Strategy: Setting Strategic Objectives

Once you've gained insight, it's time to set a primary strategic objective for each of your dual tracks.

In Exploit mode

When thinking about your strategic objectives in exploit mode you fundamentally have three choices:

- **Revenue growth** – pursuing this encourages you to move into adjacent markets and into enhancing existing new products; this can impact market share and profitability.

- **Profit growth** – focuses everyone on efficiency and making the most of available resources; it can restrict you from making significant investments in products, markets or geographical expansion.

- **Growing market share** – involves sacrificing revenue and profit in order to win lots of new customers. To take this to extremes – if you choose to give away your product for free, you will get a stronger foothold in the market. Sometimes entering a new market requires sacrificing revenue to win early deals or to gain well-known brand names as customers.

Our guidance is to choose one, and only one of these, to pursue as your primary strategic objective in exploit; the others will serve as operating constraints. For example, you might set your primary strategic objective as 30% year-on-year growth, but include as a constraint the need to maintain 10% profit.

In Explore mode

Setting your strategic objectives for explore requires a different set of disciplines, and a different mindset. On this track you're getting into new markets or developing new products and the terrain is uncertain. You will have gained experience from your existing terrain and customers, but proceed with caution and recognise that you are in learning mode.

Your strategic objective on this track should incorporate testing your assumptions in a robust and disciplined way. This will tell you what the appetite might be for your product or service in this new market. What do you need to adapt or amend? In a world where business is increasingly global, testing your assumptions in this way will save time and energy.

Due to its uncertain nature, you will probably have to 'kiss a lot of frogs' in the explore phase. Following a disciplined approach means that you will find your prince more quickly. You may not be able to set the specific revenue or profit objectives you have in exploit, but setting time-bound objectives maintains team discipline and alignment.

Gemini: Strategic Objectives

The insights garnered by the leadership team led Gemini to pursue a dual track approach of exploit and explore. They reset their objective for exploit to focus on profit growth – this was a deliberate move away from their previous strategy which had focused on revenue. They were clear about the reason: in order to raise funds to build a product for explore, they had to increase profits from their existing large-bank customers, which meant raising prices for the customised software.

On the explore track things were trickier. They wanted to test their assumption that they could use existing capabilities and knowledge to build a shrink-wrapped product for the mid-sized market. It was difficult to agree a strategic objective here because they had no track record in this market and could only speculate about what could be achieved. The strategic objective they finally settled on was: *"to win and get live three mid-sized banks with our new software product by the end of the year"*. This brought clarity around the task ahead for both the sales and engineering teams.

Gemini Strategy Statement

Industry Insight

Exploit
We believe we cannot build the company we aspire to by providing customised solutions to large banks. We cannot create real value for shareholders in this way.

Explore
We assume that there is potential for us to take our existing capabilities and knowledge to build a shrink-wrapped product for mid-sized banks.

Strategic Objectives

Exploit
Our insight has led us to a dual track approach. For our exploit track our strategic objective is to generate 15% net profit from our existing customers.

Explore
In addition, we propose to test our assumption on mid-sized banks by setting an objective to win 3 mid-sized bank customers and get them live by the end of the year.

Product/Market Scope

Competitive Advantage

3. Select the Right Strategy: Clarifying Product/Market Scope

Defining where you are going to compete, and with what products, is the most important strategy decision you will take. The right choices could have a 50% plus impact on revenue growth and profitability. Many strategies avoid, or are vague about, choices. Good strategies are clear about their scope – what are they going to sell, and to whom? They are also clear about where they are not going to compete. If you avoid these questions, you really have no strategy at all.

In Exploit Mode

Product/Market scope on your exploit track is all about seeking in-depth understanding of customer need and the benefit of your product/solution over the competition. There are two key questions:

- Who are our **Sweet Spot** customers?*
- What **Measurable Value** are we offering?*

Closing the growth gap is hard. It's even harder if you don't identify the ideal or sweet spot customers in the right market. The market always wins. Even an average team can do well if they are focused on the right sweet spot customers; conversely a great team can fail in a weak market.

Questions to consider in Exploit Mode

When thinking about **market** on your **exploit** track these questions are useful:

- How many potential customers are in this segment?
- What is the profile of our sweet spot customers?
- What industry sectors and geographies will we focus on?
- Who are our key competitors?
- What capability do we have to win?
- Will we sell directly to customers or will we sell via partners?

When thinking about **product** on your **exploit** track it's useful to ask:

- Are we primarily a product or services company?
- What products or services will we sell?
- Do we have the product features needed by our chosen market?
- Will further investment be required?
- Do we need additional resources?

*We cover both Sweet Spot customers and Measurable Value in great detail in a previous Select Strategies publication **The Business Battlecard** (Paul O'Dea, 2009). It includes tools to help you work through these questions.

In Explore Mode

Turning to the explore track, be prepared for more uncertainty. You are in discovery mode here and will probably need to test and experiment until you find the right product/market fit. Customer needs may be unarticulated and you might be profiling your ideal customer type, rather than identifying actual customers.

The key to finding your product/market scope in explore is discipline. Test your assumptions and hypotheses before you make decisive moves. Document your problem assumptions in explore. For example, Gemini's problem assumption was: *'mid-sized banks don't have the resources to procure custom-built software, so are looking for off-the-shelf solutions'.*

Questions to consider in Explore Mode

These questions are useful to investigate with potential customers:

- How motivated are the customers to solve this problem?
- How have they tried to solve it in the past?
- If they had a solution to this problem, what would that mean to them?
- If someone offered them a solution, how likely would they be to consider it?
- How much would they spend to solve that problem?
- What core capability could we leverage to enter this new market?

Gemini: Exploiting and Exploring - Product/Market Scope

Remember that exploit and explore are dual tracks and a good leadership team pursues both in tandem. All going well, explore should become your new exploit!

Gemini illustrates this well. Once they had set their strategic objective for explore – to get three customers live in the mid-sized banking sector within the year – they set about making this happen. They used the profits gained from raising their prices in exploit to build the product that mid-sized banks wanted. They were demanding: the product had to be shrink-wrapped and ready for installation 'in the cloud'; it had to be multilingual to cater to mid-sized banks globally; and it had to be delivered quickly because banks were looking for this product now.

It was a lot of work but reconfiguring their strategy and business model to deliver on their vision had lit a fire across the Gemini team. Everyone was clear about the value this new market would bring the business and they had their experience from working with larger banks to draw on. The benefits of focus were clear – Gemini got their three live customers, in Paris, Munich and San Francisco, almost on schedule.

Gemini Strategy Statement

Industry Insight

Exploit
We believe we cannot build the company we aspire to by providing customised solutions to large banks. We cannot create real value for shareholders in this way.

Explore
We assume that there is potential for us to take our existing capabilities and knowledge to build a shrink-wrapped product for mid-sized banks.

Strategic Objectives

Exploit
Our insight has led us to a dual track approach. For our exploit track our strategic objective is to generate 15% net profit from our existing customers.

Explore
In addition, we propose to test our assumption on mid-sized banks by setting an objective to win 3 mid-sized bank customers and get them live by the end of the year.

Product/Market Scope

Exploit
Focus on existing large banks to generate profits through software services projects. We will not target new large banks.

Explore
Focus on 20 mid-sized bank prospects and build a software product that is easy to use. We will invest in making this product feature-rich over time. We believe time to market is important.

Competitive Advantage

4. Select the Right Strategy: Creating Competitive Advantage

Thinking about a dual track approach, gathering insights, setting your strategic objectives and being clear on your product/market scope will set you on the path to creating a strong strategy. But the test of your strategy is whether it gives you a clear advantage over competitors.

Good strategies are clear on the competitive advantages they are going to build and on the sequence and timing of the investment required to deliver them. Great strategies often bundle a number of unique capabilities together, which makes it harder for competitors to copy them.

Being clear on your competitive advantage has a significant impact on your ability to capture value. Capturing value is about the ability of your business to generate profit from transactions. A true test of your strategy and competitive advantage in particular is whether it translates into value delivered. Businesses that struggle with articulating their competitive advantage will often find themselves competing on one criterion only – price.

The ability of a business to capture value is easily tested with one simple questions: *'Can we raise prices without losing customers?'* This question forces you to consider the strength of your competitive advantage, the barriers to entry into your industry and the quality of your revenue.

For Gemini, increasing their pricing for customised solutions in their existing market of large banks allowed them to secure enough funding to build the product for the mid-sized market.

Questions to consider on Competitive Advantage

- On what basis do your customers make selection decisions?
- Who are your key competitors?
- When do you normally win or lose against them?
- What might your competitive advantages be?
- How might you change your business model to compete, e.g. partners, pricing, who delivers what?
- What capability can you use to better advantage?
- What new capability do you need to build?

To test and improve the strength of your strategy we advise documenting your competitive advantage in a rigorous way. The aim is to validate that your perceived advantage holds up to scrutiny, and to identify areas where you need to press home your advantage.

Competitive Advantage Worksheet

In The Growth Roadmap® we use a Competitive Advantage Worksheet to help you challenge and clarify thinking. The Competitive Advantage Worksheet enables you to identify, at a glance, where the gaps are so that you can allocate resources to plug the gap and beat the competition.

- First identify the four or five criteria upon which your customers make their buying decisions. Each industry is a bit different – sample criteria include price, global reach, speed of implementation, security, quality or innovative content.

- For each of the selected criteria, rate yourself out of 10 for:
  - Where we are now?
  - What will it take to win? – Your understanding might be informed by what the customers want or where the leaders in the field are.

- The gaps between 'where we are now' and 'what will it take to win' are the areas most in need of investment.

Regularly evaluating and tweaking your Competitive Advantage Worksheet ensures strategy is a continuous process.

Gemini's Competitive Advantage Worksheet

Gemini's insight – that mid-sized banks sought cloud-based off-the-shelf products – was at the basis of the competitive advantage they developed. The team spent time debating the criteria they should use. They looked in detail at their core competencies – what were they really good at? They sought links to the buying criteria their customers used. Ultimately they agreed the following criteria would be needed to win these mid-sized customers:

- Global Reach (the product had to work in all languages)
- Ease of Use
- Banking Knowledge
- Speed of Implementation
- Depth of Features (the customers had specific demands from the product)

Gemini plotted their competitive advantage (see their Worksheet below) using these criteria to reveal gaps between their current capabilities and what new customers wanted. This revealed adequate banking knowledge and in-depth features from their work with larger customers, but they needed better ease of use and speed of implementation to deliver a global shrink-wrapped product. The focus and investment in these capabilities gave Gemini the edge and a clear competitive advantage over competitors with more muddled strategies.

The rest of the market was still supplying customised solutions when Gemini drove the mid-sized market with 'out-of-the-box' cloud-based products. Recognising that they needed to invest in closing the gaps around ease of use and speed of implementation enabled Gemini to scale rapidly. Within five years, the explore track of mid-sized banks became their new exploit, with 78 global customers.

Gemini's Competitive Advantage Worksheet

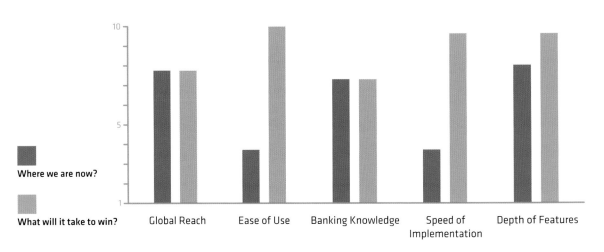

One-page Strategy Statement

The final step in Strategy is bringing all your findings and decisions together, synthesising them onto one page. Your one-page Strategy Statement communicates to the company and board how you are going to create, deliver and capture value, in existing and future markets.

Tips for creating a good Strategy Statement

A good strategy statement shapes a pattern of choices and decision-making across the business. It provides clear signposts and guides your team on what actions to take, and not to take. It is compelling and persuasive and avoids jargon and business clichés. Here are some tips to crafting your statement:

- **At the beginning ask your team to document today's actual strategy.** Clarify the exploit and explore parts of your strategy.

- **Include a timeframe.** We find that 12–18 months is a good one to use. This positions your strategy clearly in the "action now" camp, and allows you to use it as a stepping stone towards achieving your shared vision.

- **Be clear.** It should make clear what the business has chosen to do and not to do, and why those decisions were taken.

- **Provide clarity on resource allocation and investment choices.**

- **Be co-ordinated.** A good strategy statement pulls the different strands of the business together, so everyone is facing the same direction and is clear about their common goals.

- **Connect broad goals and detailed actions.** This will make it easier to form a bridge between the broad high-level goals and the on-the-ground actions that can deliver those goals.

- **If your business has many business units then this same model can be adapted to cater for a corporate/business unit structure.**

- **Finally, test the logic of your strategy statement.** How ambitious is it? How realistic? Is the reasoning for your competitive advantage sound?

Strategy Statement

You and your team have now discussed, investigated and completed a number of worksheet exercises on Industry Insight, Strategic Objectives, Product/Market Scope and Competitive Advantage. To finalise, pull together a synthesis of these discussions and choices into your Strategy Statement. The Gemini sample below will provide guidance on approach and format.

 # Gemini Strategy Statement

Industry Insight

Exploit
We believe we cannot build the company we aspire to by providing customised solutions to large banks. We cannot create real value for shareholders in this way.

Explore
We assume that there is potential for us to take our existing capabilities and knowledge to build a shrink-wrapped product for mid-sized banks.

Strategic Objectives

Exploit
Our insight has led us to a dual track approach. For our exploit track our strategic objective is to generate 15% net profit from our existing customers.

Explore
In addition, we propose to test our assumption on mid-sized banks by setting an objective to win 3 mid-sized bank customers and get them live by the end of the year.

Product/Market Scope

Exploit
Focus on existing large banks to generate profits through software services projects. We will not target new large banks.

Explore
Focus on 20 mid-sized bank prospects and build a software product that is easy to use. We will invest in making this product feature-rich over time. We believe time to market is important.

Competitive Advantage

Exploit
Our existing competitive advantage is based on banking knowledge and in-depth features from our work with larger customers. We will continue to invest in these capabilities in the short term.

Explore
Our future competitive advantage will be based on ease of use and speed of implementation. We will invest in both of these capabilities.

We include a blank Strategy Statement in the Worksheets section for you to complete your own.

"It is only by saying no that you can concentrate on the things that are really important".

STEVE JOBS

Stage 4. Overcome Scaling Challenges

Virgo has been a client of ours for a number of years. When we first met, they had been through a couple of difficult years sparked by an economic downturn. Today revenue has grown to over €300m and Virgo has utterly transformed.

Virgo builds telecoms infrastructure that is applicable to a broad range of industries. When we first met, they were targeting five diverse industries. The cry from the sales team was that products were too expensive and they couldn't compete. Their value proposition was unclear and sales cycles were long and unpredictable.

The development of a clear and compelling strategy statement was a key turning point for Virgo. Having diagnosed the root causes behind their long sales cycles and the continuous downward pressure on pricing, they took the decision to refocus on a particular market segment – Tier 1 technology companies – who didn't care so much about pricing but valued Virgo's quality product. These customers wanted the *Rolls-Royce* product and were prepared to pay for it.

On paper this sounds straightforward: change the strategy, focus on a new market segment and bingo the business grows by 10x in five years. But real life is seldom so straightforward. This change in strategic direction represented a major shift for Virgo, which affected every part of their business – from sales to delivery, from the factory floor to accounts.

These changes meant that Virgo's leadership team was confronted with a set of challenges around strategy execution. Some of the scaling challenges involved issues they were already aware of, like the need to improve the sales process, others were challenges specific to the new strategy direction.

For instance, the new target customers, Tier 1 technology companies, were global players with high standards who demanded the same from suppliers, so Virgo would have to greatly improve customer service. This involved driving a whole new set of behaviours across the company.

The leadership team was daunted but determined. They believed in the strategy. They had communicated their ambition to aggressively scale the business to their staff and the board. But they realised that their strategy statement would remain just that – a statement – unless they put in the work to execute it, addressing the challenges in a disciplined and targeted way.

Scaling challenges are the engine room of growth

In Stage 3, Select the Right Strategy, we look at **what** you need to do to transform growth. In Stage 4, Overcome Scaling Challenges, we look at **how** you will do this. Your Strategy Statement is a statement of intent, based on a deep understanding and exploration of your business and industry. The next step is to deliver on that intention. Acting on the decisions you have taken in strategy can have deep consequences across the company. The larger the company, the more complex and significant those consequences.

Many companies create long lists of actions to deliver a strategy, an approach which more often than not produces disappointing results. In The Growth Roadmap© we propose a more prioritised approach, focusing on the critical few challenges that need to be overcome in the next two to three quarters to deliver the strategy.

Scaling challenges are the engine room of growth. They start to translate the strategy into reality, and make the abstract concrete. Getting this right typically involves more than the leadership team. The wider organisation starts to see the strategy come to life.

Businesses that scale well have the ability to accelerate revenue growth without having to increase costs rapidly. For example:

- A business in a small competitive market may find it easier to scale by entering into a large growing market

- A 'software as a service' or cloud-based technology business can scale rapidly as the incremental cost of acquiring and onboarding new customers is normally modest

- A service business can scale by having disciplined processes that do not rely on key individuals

- An overstretched Founder CEO may find it easier to scale the business, if he hires a Chief Operations Officer (COO).

Lack of scalability is at the root cause of the growth gap. The Growth Roadmap© provides a cohesive approach to business scaling across four dimensions: market, product, leadership and performance.

The scaling challenge process takes what may have seemed insurmountable and breaks it down into smaller focused chunks. It introduces a common language and set of visual tools, which help collaborative problem solving and critical thinking. We find that clients often continue to use this approach well after they've finished working through The Growth Roadmap©.

Selecting your Scaling Challenges

Working through the first three stages of The Growth Roadmap®, you will have gathered a ton of data and gained in-depth understanding of your company and industry. Now it's a matter of prioritisation to select your scaling challenges.

It's interesting, you would think that asking all team members to suggest three scaling challenges would lead to a long laundry list. But we've done this exercise with teams over 100 times and in 90% of cases a clear set of themes emerges relatively quickly.

In one case a client insisted on developing 10 challenges, with a leadership team of four. Even trying to remember what the challenges were was a "challenge" for us all. The results were predictable – three or four of the challenges got all the attention (rightly so). However, this left the team feeling dejected, as they were constantly reminded of those they 'failed' to deliver on.

It's best to choose between three and five company scaling challenges. Force yourselves to focus – what are the small number of challenges, which if addressed, could really move the dial and enable scale? If you need to prioritise, seek balanced dialogue.

Finally, as you start selecting your key scaling challenges it's useful to reflect back on the work done on Diagnosis, Shared Vision and Strategy. Too often teams focus on growth when they should be focused on scale. Keep in mind the difference between the two.

Growth can be expensive. In The Growth Roadmap®, we look for ways to scale businesses or grow them as efficiently as possible. A good way to make your business scalable is to identify the parts that can grow quickly without generating too much additional cost. For instance, an internet based software product – once created, all subsequent copies are cheap to produce.

Scalability requires some degree of standardisation. It may mean stopping certain activities. New processes may enable repeatability and scalability. Being able to scale up helps mid-sized businesses become big businesses without incurring the ballooning costs that might be required for aggressive growth.

Selecting your Scaling Challenges – Exercise

- Ask team members to take some time to reflect on what they believe are the key scaling challenges.

- Take input on thinking from the previous stages of The Growth Roadmap®.

- When you've gathered the team ask each member to succinctly write their identified challenges onto a post-it – one idea per post-it note.

- Invite each team member, one at a time, to put their post-it note up on the board/flipchart, outlining to the group the logic behind their choice.

- Seek to understand both their logic and emotional reasoning behind their choices.

- Once you have everyone's post-it up, group and sort them by theme.

- Think about balance between different areas of the business. Are all the selected challenges focused on sales? Have we forgotten about product?

- Discuss and debate whether the challenges you select will deliver a significant impact. Ask how addressing these challenges will deliver your strategy and scale your business.

- Finally, once you have reached your decision, assign one team member as the accountable owner for the challenge. They will be responsible for driving the challenge through the three steps of the scaling challenge process.

Stage 4. Overcome Scaling Challenges

Now you have selected your scaling challenges you are ready to start working on them. **There are three steps in the scaling challenge stage:**

1.  Defining Scaling Challenges

2. Proposing Solutions

3. Crafting your Scaling Scorecard

1.  Overcome Scaling Challenges: Defining Scaling Challenges

Albert Einstein famously said that if he had one hour to save the world he would spend 55 minutes defining the problem and five minutes finding the solution. That's a nicely hyperbolic way of getting across that a thorough understanding of the problem is required before an effective solution can be found.

There is often a strong urge to rush past this stage. Team members believe they know the problem or the root cause of the challenges they face. However, often they have only looked at the symptoms. In order to ask the right question it's important to put in the work.

Make your Scaling Challenge SMART

The first step is to take the agreed challenge and frame it into a SMART question. SMART stands for specific, measurable, achievable, relevant and time-bound. Good SMART questions start with 'how' or 'what'. They take a bit of practice to get right but when well-crafted they are easy to remember, bring the challenge to life, and motivate action.

The strength of the scaling challenge process is that it can be used in all major business areas – market, product, leadership and performance.

Here are some examples of well crafted SMART Scaling Challenge questions:

- How do we become a high performing leadership team within 12 months?

- How will we scale international sales to enable us to double revenue within 3 years?

- How do we increase the rate of new feature delivery in our product by at least 30% within six months?

- What do we need to do to reduce product delivery costs by 20% within 12 months?

- What can we do to ensure buy-in to the product roadmap process within 6 months?

- How will we digitise our business over the next 24 months?

- How will we double revenue from existing customers within the next 18 months?

At the start of this chapter we met Virgo, their key strategic decision to change sweet spot had left them with a set of scaling challenges. One of those was crafted into the SMART question– *'How can we deliver 80% of revenue from the Tier 1 technology market within three years?'*

Stage 4. Overcome Scaling Challenges

Once the question is defined it's time to look at the remaining parts of the definition worksheet:

1. **Situation**
   What is the current external and internal situation? Why is this currently important? What might happen if we don't address the situation?

2. **Complication**
   Why haven't we solved this issue before? What is at the root cause? What might get in the way of addressing it? What political, personal or other implications are there?

3. **Scope**
   What will (and will not) be included? What is the scope of the proposed challenge? What are we going to focus on? What are we going to exclude from scope?

4. **Capability to execute**
   Do we have the right people with the right skill-set to address the challenge? Do we have the necessary financial resources? Is there ambition and drive to deliver?

5. **Key sources of insight**
   What expertise could help us address the challenge? You improve the speed, agility and innovativeness of your problem solving when you seek out alternative perspectives.

6. **Criteria for success**
   What does 'good' look like by a specific date? Set out criteria for success to motivate and guide direction. Select KPIs to measure progress.

Our Virgo team had selected the issue of stagnant sales as one of the prioritised scaling challenges. To achieve ambitious new growth targets and a new focus on the Tier 1 technology market would require successful entry into the US market. Whilst the team agreed this was the right market, there was less alignment on the best way to enter the US and grow sales.

As an added complication, leadership team bonuses were tied to profit, which resulted in caution on investing in sales. The team knew they had to move beyond the blame game of talking about 'fixing the sales problem' to a more focused challenge definition. Their SMART question evolved to *'how can we deliver 80% of revenue from the Tier 1 technology market within three years?'* The Scaling Challenge Worksheet helped them do a deep dive to uncover the root causes of the issue.

Let's take a look at the worksheet which will help you through the scaling challenge process.

Scaling Challenge Worksheet – Define

You and your team can use the Scaling Challenge Worksheet below to clarify and document the scaling challenges you have chosen. The Virgo example should guide you. It's best to document an initial draft relatively quickly and have team reviews to ensure clarity and commitment.

 # Virgo Scaling Challenge Worksheet

How can we deliver 80% of revenue from the Tier 1 technology market within three years?

1. Situation

The Tier 1 technology market is growing rapidly and we have a great opportunity to benefit from it. We have existing customers in that segment, they want more product from us and we have a good pipeline of new prospects. But competitors are growing rapidly.

4. Capability to execute

We have limited market data and sales coverage is low. The board is not yet convinced we can deliver. We need 3 new sales hires to focus on new customer wins in this market.

2. Complication

We have changed to a higher demanding market sector. As a leadership team, we have not grasped the requirement to professionalise and invest in our sales and delivery systems. This is partly a mindset gap – we don't know what the bar is. Also, our bonuses are tied to profit, so we are cautious about investing in new systems.

5. Key sources of insight

John Doe really understands this market. He has extensive US experience. Ten days with him would help validate our assumptions. We could also learn a lot more by speaking with our existing customers.

3. Scope

We will only focus on the US market for our sweet spot clients. Only products that are currently on our approved product roadmap will be included. We will not consider the partner channel for now.

6. Criteria for success

Leadership team and board alignment. Move from 30%, year-on-year growth this year to 50% growth next year. Quick wins through upselling to existing customers.

2. Overcome Scaling Challenges: Proposing Solutions

Now that you've done a robust job of defining your Scaling Challenges, it's time to start thinking about solutions. Think of this stage as brainstorming. You're not selecting or taking decisions yet; you're putting potential solutions on the table. Examine them, debate them with the team and then decide which to take forward.

The Solutions Worksheet is great for this. It allows you propose an option, expand it into some level of detail and then either choose to stick with it, or abandon it for another option. There are many ways to solve a challenge, the solutions worksheet helps you uncover the most effective and efficient solution. Remember you are in brainstorming mode here – try not to rule things in or out too quickly. Use the worksheet to help structure your thinking.

It's helpful to work from left to right. Start with the SMART question you defined in the Scaling Challenge Worksheet. Then use the next two layers of the worksheet to start exploring solutions.

Our guidance is to only allow three proposed solutions through to the next stage. Again, the mantra here is focus. Forcing yourself to limit the solutions drives the right conversations with the team and avoids the team ending up with an inexecutable laundry list of action items to tackle.

The worksheet enables you to present each challenge in a visible structure that can be readily grasped by all team members. This makes it easier to align around a common understanding and the proposed paths to addressing it.

Look to strike a balance between addressing urgent issues and working on the longer term important issues. Some solutions will have higher impact, where others will be easier to implement.

The Virgo team came up with a number of proposed solutions to their *'How can we deliver 80% of revenue from Tier 1 technology market within three years'* challenge. They whittled them down to three:

- Upsell to existing customers
- Win new customers
- Introduce new product

Solutions Worksheet – Structuring the Challenge

Proposing solutions using the tree structure below enables you and your team to brainstorm and document different options to address your scaling challenge. The Virgo example below will help guide your approach. The single page visual tree helps focus on a limited number of initiatives to maximise impact.

Virgo Solutions Worksheet

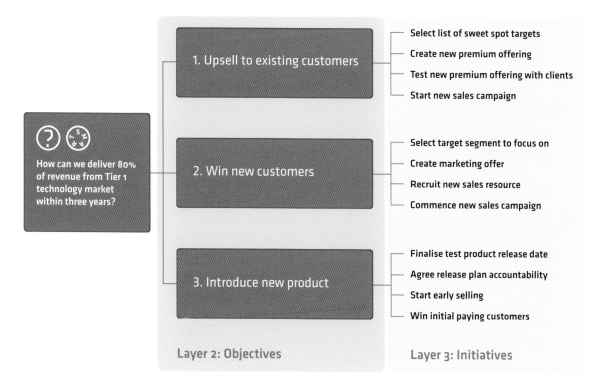

Some tips on completing Solutions Worksheet

1. **Use the thinking done in your Scaling Challenge Worksheet to inform this task**. For most challenges, there are a number of ways to structure the proposed solutions. In the Virgo example the solutions are: a) Upsell to existing customers, b) Win new customers, and c) Introduce new product. Another way to have structured this Solutions Worksheet might have been by territory: a) Penetrate US Market, b) Introduce new product to EMEA and c) Acquire company in Asia.

2. **Use the Solutions Worksheet to help structure your team's best thinking.** Think through the best options to address the challenge in an optimal way. Use a flip-chart with your team to help craft the Solutions Worksheet.

3. **Layer 2 – Objectives:** We structure the Solutions Worksheet with three objectives at the next layer. Objectives are goals (no more than three) that, if accomplished, will enable your company to overcome the scaling challenge. When you create an objective, focus hard on what the challenge is trying to accomplish. Sequence your objectives logically. See 'Upsell to existing customers' in the example. We recommend using one verb and two nouns for all objectives. Make sure that the objective title is clear.

4. **Layer 3 – Initiatives:** At the next layer, after objectives are initiatives. We define initiatives as projects or major actions. Sequence your initiatives logically. There should be less than five initiatives for each objective. These initiatives should focus on the next quarter or two. Keep initiative descriptions short – again use one verb and two or three nouns.

5. Doing the work well on your Solutions Worksheet will make completing your Scaling Scorecard much more straightforward. Try to prioritise so that your worksheet includes the objectives and intiatives that provide the highest impact, with the least effort.

3. Overcome Scaling Challenges: Crafting your Scaling Scorecard

The final stage of this scaling challenge process shifts the focus to execution. We use a Scaling Scorecard to translate the scaling challenge into reality and to put sustainable and considered solutions in place.

The Scaling Scorecard helps translate challenges into operational reality. Clearly stated initiatives and timelines mean everyone knows what needs to happen, and when. The scorecard provides an easy way to keep all employees abreast of and committed to addressing these important challenges.

The visual nature of the scorecard is important. Keeping everything on one page makes it easier to digest - and if you think about what might be happening across three or four challenges concurrently, this is important. We suggest using a single page view, regardless of the tool e.g. Powerpoint, Google Docs etc.

Regular reviews of your scorecard later on drives momentum. Progress is visible and you can iterate through the initiatives as you make progress.

Finally, the work done on your solutions worksheet provides your starting point and thinking to inform your scorecard.

Understanding the Scaling Scorecard

The Scaling Scorecard is presented in a simple table structure and for each challenge sets out the following:

Objectives
These are the goals (no more than three) that, if accomplished, will enable your company to meet the challenge.

Measures
Select two measures that can be used to track progress towards meeting each objective.

Targets
The targets you will set against each measure to keep progress on track.

Initiatives
These are the priority actions, or groupings of actions (no more than five), that need to be taken to ensure the objectives can be realised.

Scaling Scorecard

For Virgo, the challenge *"How can we deliver 80% of revenue from Tier 1 technology market within three years?"* started the team on a disciplined process to work through the three components of their scaling challenge – upsell to existing customers, new customer wins and a new product launch. The planning process showed them a high level path and made it easier to agree the targets and initiatives that would drive them forward.

Virgo Scaling Scorecard:

How can we deliver 80% of revenue from Tier 1 technology market within three years?

John Smith, *Sales and Marketing*

Objectives	Measures	Targets	Initiatives
1. Upsell to existing customers	• Avg revenue per customer /per quarter	Today (€50k) Target end Q1 (€55k)	1. Select list of sweet spot target customers (JC, wk 1)
			2. Create new premium offering (PC, wk 3)
	• No. of accounts with commissioned sales person	Today (30) Target end Q1 (47)	3. Test new premium offering with selected customers (PC, wk 6)
			4. Agree new sales training/bonus plan (JC, wk 7)
			5. Implement new sales campaign (JC, wk 8)
2. Win new customers	• No. of new customers won	Today (2) Target end Q1 (5)	1. Select target segment to focus on (JC, wk 1)
			2. Create marketing offer (PC, wk2)
			3. Recruit new sales resource (JC, wk3)
	• No. of new sales qualified leads	Today (5) Target end Q1 (53)	4. Test marketing offer with small sample (JC, wk 5)
			5. Implement new sales campaign (JC, wk 8)
3. **Introduce new product**	• No. of test customers	Today (0) Target end Q1 (5)	1. Finalise test product release date (CG, wk 2)
			2. Agree release plan accountability (EOD, wk 3)
			3. Publish marketing collateral (COD, wk 4)
	• No. of paying customers	Today (0) Target end Q1 (2)	4. Start early test selling (RG, wk 4)
			5. Win initial paying customers (EOD, wk 10)

We have included a blank Scaling Scorecard in the Worksheets section for you to complete your own.

Building a robust set of scorecards is a critical success factor when it comes to strategy execution. Working through these with clients over the years we've learnt a few ways to get the best from the scorecard approach.

On Objectives

- Start with the second layer from your solutions worksheet. Use the work done here as the basis for your objectives. For Virgo the work done on the solutions worksheet left them with three objectives – upsell to existing customers, win new customers, introduce new product.

On Measures

- Keep it simple. Ideally you should have no more than two measures per objective.

- Effective measures are well-defined and quantifiable. Most importantly they should be aligned with your overall strategy.

- Choose measures that are in line with your broader business level KPIs (we come to this in the next stage).

- Try to keep a balance between 'lead' and 'lag' measures – see panel below.

On Targets

- The targets defined should link directly to the measures identified. In Virgo's case they set a measure of quarterly revenue per customer, and a target of €55k for the end of the quarter for that measure.

- Encourage your team to set targets that are challenging, but that don't overstretch too much. Plan some early wins.

On Initiatives

- Use the thinking done in the third layer of your solutions worksheet to inform this section. For example, Virgo had identified 'Selection of target segment' in their worksheet. This then carried over to their Scaling Scorecard once the team had agreed it was the right initiative.

- Resist the temptation to pile everything needed to meet the objective into the first quarter of the plan. Summarise the initiatives across all challenges on a calendarised chart to create a picture of what is happening when across the organisation.

Some tips on completing Scaling Scorecards

'Lead measures' predict future performance and act like early warning systems – for example customer service. 'Lag measures' report on what has already happened and act like a rear view mirror on performance – for example revenue and sales.

Lead and lag measures

90

"However beautiful the strategy, you should occasionally measure the results".

WINSTON CHURCHILL

Capricorn

Capricorn is a large software services company selling software to many different industries.

A client of ours, Capricorn, is a software services company. We first met the CEO, at her request, in her office one evening. She had asked us to get involved quite late in the growth planning process, after the team had agreed a strategy and were starting to implement it. But things weren't going the way they'd hoped. She pointed ruefully to a binder on her desk:

"It's all in there," she said, *"We had a top four consulting firm in and we've put together a clear growth plan. It's a strong plan but performance isn't improving! My whole team signed up to this but now they seem disengaged from delivering. The board are starting to ask questions. It's so frustrating, I don't get it".*

We understood her frustration – no improvement in performance after all that work! But we were able to reassure her. We hear variations of her story frequently.

At this stage of strategy execution, it's not uncommon for companies to experience a disconnect between intent and follow-through. A chasm seems to appear between the leadership team's goals and the capability of the organisation to achieve them. In desperation the leadership team starts scheduling off-sites, which don't really change the dynamic.

None of this means that there's any inherent weakness in the team or the strategy. Look on it as an early warning sign that you probably need to put in place a process to keep growth on track and avoid drift. Scaling means letting go of long-held beliefs and ways of doing things and this involves getting used to new behaviours. This isn't easy and the default for companies, like people, is to revert to the status quo.

The key to staying focused on your goals is to continually monitor progress along the route and to learn what's working and what's not. Think of it like Weight Watchers – you can put together the perfect diet and exercise plan, but it's the weekly public weigh-in that makes you stick to the plan.

What gets measured, gets done. If the public weigh-in reveals no change or, worse, weight gain, you're motivated to get back on track with the programme. If the weigh-in reveals weight loss, you're inspired to do even better.

Measuring results is such an essential part of growth transformation that ideally it would be incorporated, in a disciplined way, into every business strategy. We should all learn from Weight Watchers. Doing the hard planning work and then not putting in place tools to measure progress is the very definition of falling at the last hurdle.

Most leadership teams understand intuitively the importance of monitoring progress. They become enthusiastic about incorporating metrics – particularly because the scheduled 'weigh-in' sessions generate momentum. However, getting to a balanced set of metrics can be tricky.

The challenge for senior teams is to agree on the key performance metrics that affect the business and to align these to the strategy. A danger that many teams fall into is focusing solely on the financial metrics – neglecting the fact that effective scaling involves all areas within a company.

In Capricorn's case, we found that their strategy included ambitions about customer service that weren't being measured in any quantifiable way. Their strategic assumptions also included increasing revenue from existing customers, but this wasn't being tracked by the CFO's reports. The CEO had an excess of financial data, but it wasn't being linked to the strategy.

In this final stage of The Growth Roadmap©, we provide tools to measure results that enable leadership teams to monitor strategy execution, focus alignment and improve communication of the strategy across the whole company. **We suggest three key steps:**

1. **Summary Financial Model**

Ensuring the whole team understands the Summary Financial Model and the levers that impact performance.

2. **Business KPI Model**

Measuring progress by ensuring there is a clear KPI model that shows how all components of the business dovetail to deliver performance.

3.  **Performance Rhythm**

Establishing a clear Performance Rhythm to ensure good, open conversations which keep performance on track.

1. Keep Growth on Track: Summary Financial Model

The objective in building your Summary Financial Model is to make clear how your proposed strategy links to the financials to help evaluate progress and learn what is working and what might need to be changed. Your Summary Financial Model should tell the story of the strategy in a language that everyone can understand.

All too often we meet teams where financial information is hidden or overly detailed. These teams may be deluged with financial data but if the data isn't clearly connected to the strategic assumptions and objectives, then it isn't measuring results and it's probably contributing to a sense of overload and confusion.

In our work with Capricorn, a pivotal moment occurred during a discussion with the CFO on revenue numbers. We asked what the average quota per sales person was. The CFO was curious as to why we wanted to know. We pointed out that based on the numbers, it looked like Capricorn would need 50+ sales people to deliver that revenue number. Currently they only had 10, which felt like a very big jump.

Documenting the assumption which underpinned the numbers – i.e. 50 sales people delivering average annual revenue of X – brought to light a disconnect between the head of sales and the CFO. To deliver the revenue numbers the sales team would need to grow from 10 to 50. However, the head of sales was focused on achieving the current year's numbers. To deliver the projected numbers, growing the team was a pressing issue that couldn't be ignored.

The Capricorn team looked in detail at the resource investment required to deliver the sales numbers. They then incorporated that investment into their financial model. It was clear then that they would require significant additional funding to realise their growth ambitions.

Questions to consider in your Summary Financial Model

Before you start working on your Summary Financial Model, here are some questions to reflect on:

- Where does your business really make money – both gross margin and profit? How does it compare to similar type or sized companies?

- What do the trends in your financial model tell you about how well business is performing?

- What are key performance trends and critical risks?

- What are key levers to improve performance?

- What is the size of the growth gap?

- How scalable is the existing financial model? What are the key risks? What sensitivity analysis should be done?

- What key actions would you recommend?

- How well does each member of your leadership team understand the financial model and their part in improving performance?

- What funding might be required to deliver the plan? Can this be secured on terms that are acceptable? What proof points or milestones would need to be achieved to secure funding on the right terms?

Documenting in words the assumptions that underpin the numbers can be a truly transformative exercise – providing clarity for all, and allowing the non-financial people on the team to stress-test the numbers as well. Here are some suggestions to consider:

Tips: Documenting Assumptions and Finalising your Summary Financial Model

- Simplify your financial model down to the five or 10 financial numbers that are most important – e.g. revenue, gross margin, growth rates, profit etc. This may involve grouping categories – i.e. putting items like salaries and overheads into 'operating expenses'. Define precisely what is meant by each category to ensure clarity.

- Consider what targets you should be setting for key financial ratios if you are to achieve your strategy and shared vision.

- Document the assumption you are making beside each financial metric e.g. revenue growth at 45% year-on-year. Make these assumptions both challenging and realistic using inputs from your strategy, past trends and top quartile peer companies.

- Identify and document the critical risks in your plan. Capture a way of monitoring these – e.g. if the assumption is that sales will be €3 million per year, include a monitor on sales pipeline.

- Include the most insightful or key financial ratios, trends e.g. growth of sales, gross margin/sales.

- Seek to express the strategy through the number. If your strategic objective for the coming year is to focus on entering a new market, then the revenue and costs associated with this should be clearly visible to all through the financial model.

- Finally link your summary financial model appropriately to your shared vision stretch number.

Every business will use a slightly different model or layout for their Summary Financial Model. Below we show Capricorn's – yours may have different metrics. Note the guidance given earlier in this chapter on clarity, simplicity and the documenting of assumptions.

Capricorn's Simplified Summary Financial Model

Summary P&L	Last year	Current year	Plan year 1	Plan year 2	Plan year 3
Revenue	€13m	€16m	€23m	€31m	€45m
Revenue – existing customers	€5m	€6m	€7m	€9m	€10m
Revenue – new customers	€8m	€10m	€13m	€17m	€23m
Revenue – new products	–	–	€3m	€5m	€12m
Operational Expenses	€10m	€18m	€24m	€25m	€35m
Net Profit	€3m	(€2m)	(€1m)	€6m	€10m
Cash	€3m	€1m	(0)	€6m	€16m

Key Financial Assumptions

- Revenue growth will increase by over 40% per annum for next 3 years
- Sales to existing customers will grow at 20% approx per annum
- Sales to new customers will grow at approx 30% per annum
- New products revenue assumes successful launch
- Substantial increase in operating expenses from product and sales investment.

We include a blank Summary Financial Model in the Worksheets section for you to complete your own.

2. Keep Growth on Track: Business KPI Model

Capricorn had a history of growing through acquisition. Over the years, their structure had become complicated and their systems made it difficult to get data. What data they did have was exceptionally detailed and focused only on the financials.

Capricorn were in a number of markets and their biggest market was becoming commoditised. They didn't find this out through the financial data – it was only when they looked at customer usage patterns and satisfaction that they discovered product usage was trending down.

We identified Capricorn's challenge as, first, to build a model that enabled them to start measuring more than just financial results. Second, to ensure that this system faced forwards and backwards by including 'lead measures' to predict future performance and 'lag measures' to report on what had already happened. In short, Capricorn needed a good KPI model.

A clear, well balanced KPI model provides a set of navigation instruments so that the team know at all times whether they are on or off track. It provides a language to help communicate strategy. For example, the statement 'we love our customers' is laudable, but implementing a customer net promoter score to measure how loved your customers actually feel is actionable.

Questions to consider in your Business KPI Model

Before you gather the team to work on your Business KPI model here are some questions to reflect on:

- What are the key performance questions you and your senior leadership team need to understand to better measure company performance?

- What additional key performance questions might you need answers for, based on The Growth Roadmap® process?

- What key performance metrics do your leadership team find most useful today?

- Which performance metrics no longer apply?

- Which ones do you review at board meetings?

- What are current operational or departmental metrics?

- What is the process and who needs to be involved in selecting the top 5-10 business level KPIs?

Developing your Business KPI Model

KPIs work like the dials on a compass or a dashboard, letting all team members know where they are, where they are going and whether they are on course to meet their targets.

Good business KPIs should measure execution of your strategy. For example, if a strategic objective is 'the customer is king' then you might consider the following:

- **Financial:** Annual recurring revenue

- **Customer:** Customer satisfaction or revenue per customer

- **Product:** New product introductions

- **People:** Employee satisfaction.

Try to include measures across the four key company areas. The underlying philosophy is that if people develop and deliver products which customers find valuable, then financial results will follow. Using the four key company areas to document your KPIs enables you to consider the business as a whole – not just the financial results.

Finally, assigning ownership is a crucial factor in driving execution of your chosen strategy. The best results often come when each KPI is assigned an individual owner. In Appendix 4, we provide sample KPIs across the key company areas.

Review your strategy statement and your scaling challenges to guide what you should measure, and you can also use metrics already in place, if appropriate. Consider whether your chosen business KPIs meet the following criteria:

Team Exercise for building your Business KPI Model

- Do the chosen business KPIs help describe your stated strategy?

- Do they tell the story of what matters?

- Does your KPI chart illustrate a cohesive strategy and the cause and effect of that strategy?

- Does it help align different teams across the business?

Make it visual: consider developing a visual template for your KPI model, which might use colours, traffic lights, a count-down clock etc. This allows everyone to see, at a glance, what the metrics are and whether they are being delivered.

Note: When selecting business level KPIs, keep them high level enough that they measure overall business performance. In addition to these KPIs, your company may have more detailed operational or departmental KPIs. These should feed up to those at business level.

Capricorn's KPI Model

Before charting their KPIs on a model visually, Capricorn worked with us to identify the key assumptions and strategic objectives underpinning the model. These included the following for the coming year:

1. Improve cross-sell of additional products to existing customers by 10%

2. Improve product usage by 18%

3. Increase recurring revenue year-on-year by 20%

4. Acquire 10 new sweet spot customers by year end

5. Improve customer net promoter score by 15% – so that we can upsell additional products and services and get more referrals

6. Improve employee net promoter score by 12%.

Outlining their key assumptions and strategic objectives was important. Their KPI model would need to reflect these and ensure that the right elements of the business were being measured in order to achieve their goals.

Capricorn's Business KPI Model

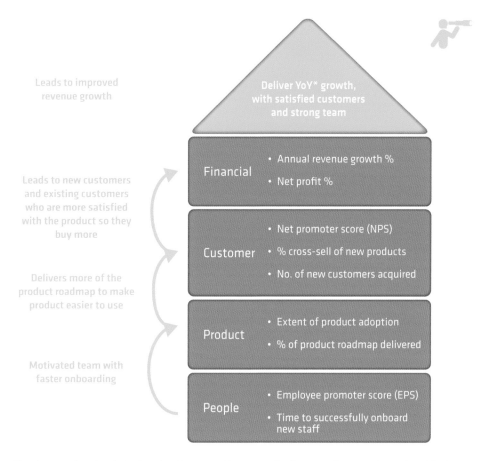

Leads to improved
revenue growth

Deliver YoY* growth,
with satisfied customers
and strong team

Financial
- Annual revenue growth %
- Net profit %

Leads to new customers
and existing customers
who are more satisfied
with the product so they
buy more

Customer
- Net promoter score (NPS)
- % cross-sell of new products
- No. of new customers acquired

Delivers more of the
product roadmap to make
product easier to use

Product
- Extent of product adoption
- % of product roadmap delivered

Motivated team with
faster onboarding

People
- Employee promoter score (EPS)
- Time to successfully onboard new staff

Capricorn prioritised the key business performance indicators down to just nine. Their leadership team really focused relentlessly on these. Everyone in the company became aware of their importance and how their department and personal objectives contributed. This process helped Capricorn close the growth gap and scale, through implementing a performance rhythm.

YoY – Year-on-year

We include a blank Business KPI Model in the Worksheets section for you to complete your own.

3. Keep Growth on Track: Performance Rhythm

At the heart of any drive for scale or growth lies a change in the way the leadership team works. This may require a new and improved rhythm of assessing performance and measuring results. Ideally, think about scheduling structured sessions so that the team can step back from the whirlwind of the day-to-day.

Your Summary Financial and Business KPI Models provide the metrics needed to measure results and learning. The final step is the 'weigh-in' – establishing a performance rhythm to ensure that you regularly take the time to monitor these metrics in a smooth and streamlined way.

A good performance rhythm doesn't just happen naturally – it needs to be scheduled, structured and documented. It becomes part of the mindset shift needed to transform growth. Eventually the rhythm becomes part of the way your company works and scales successfully.

No doubt, you already have a series of meetings scheduled. Some of your team probably protest that you have too many – it's unlikely they are asking for more! But a good performance rhythm isn't necessarily about scheduling more meetings with more team members.

Ask yourself: Can we use our existing meetings in a more targeted way? Are we involving too many people – who really needs to be in the room? Is the environment conducive to taking a hard look at strategy implementation? Would it help to have meetings off-site?

Building a Quarterly Performance Rhythm Chart

We suggest plotting out your preferred performance rhythm on a single slide. Set it out quarterly. The slide should integrate all the company's senior level meetings into something cohesive.

For each type of meeting – e.g. operational management, R&D, customer service, board – the chart should plot out the purpose, the attendees, the frequency, and a section entitled 'Review Focus'.

The chart shows visually what will happen each quarter. It ensures that people know what to expect, and when. It flags what's important to different teams and departments. Try to sequence meetings so they feed into each other. For example, the head of sales may decide on weekly meetings, which may feed into reports for the senior leadership team. This makes the cadence and rhythm clearer to all and more productive as the right data is available more readily.

Making the purpose of each meeting explicit clarifies to attendees what to expect. Is it a meeting to communicate information? To review progress and apply corrective action? To solve problems? To take decisions?

Having a clearly documented performance rhythm is a key factor when it comes to scaling. It significantly improves communication up and down the company. It clarifies responsibility. The team, rather than just the leader, start to hold each other accountable. It gives people the opportunity to support each other, to learn and to perform like a real team.

Quick Wins

Companies that identify **quick wins** or early milestones create momentum in their strategy execution plans. Examine your execution plans carefully and look for quick wins. Identify them, call them out clearly to the team. When the win is achieved, celebrate the heck out of it! The virtuous circle and momentum that is generated can truly be a driving force.

If Capricorn's leadership team had one complaint, it was 'too many meetings!' One of the leaders suggested humorously that she spent so much time in meetings, she wasn't sure she was actually doing any work!

We sat down with the team to document the existing set of meetings in the calendar. After we had clarified the purpose of each meeting and the attendance, it became clear that some people were scheduled to attend meetings they didn't need to be at. Conversely, because Capricorn is a large company and the leadership team is geographically spread, key members of the team weren't always available when issues relevant to them were being discussed.

Frequently meetings were for information-sharing only rather than decision-making. Attendees found this frustrating, feeling rightly that there were other ways to share information. It became clear that these frustrations and those of the CEO around speed of strategy implementation had similar root causes.

Capricorn changed their whole approach. They documented what meetings were happening, what the purpose was and who was attending. This revealed a pattern of too many meetings, too many attendees and too much information sharing. They rationalised their whole approach. Capricorn now has a streamlined rhythm, which is having a positive impact on their ability to scale.

Performance Rhythm Chart – Capricorn

Meeting	Purpose	Attendees	Frequency	Review Focus
Board	Shareholder support and input	Board, CEO, Mgmt team by invite	Q	Business Performance
Senior Leadership Team	Alignment, decision-making	SLT	F	Business KPIs/Financial Performance
Sales	Sales execution and pipeline review	Sales team, CEO	F	Operational Sales KPIs
Services Monthly Management	Review of key deliverables	Ops team leads	F	Client delivery
R&D Management	Review of R&D key deliverables	Head of Product, Head of Eng, CTO	F	Product Roadmap Product Velocity/Challenge
Staff Townhall	Communications progress	SLT, all staff	Q	Mindset shift, employee recognition, quick wins, focus for next quarter

Q = Quarterly, F = Fortnightly

We have included a blank Performance Rhythm Chart in the Worksheets section for you to complete your own.

"It's not the destination, it's the journey that counts".

RALPH WALDO EMERSON

Conclusion

Earlier in the book we met Virgo (Stage 4) who were confronting the scaling challenges resulting from the key strategic decision to refocus the business on the Tier 1 technology market. At the time revenue was hovering around the €20m mark. Here we share their approach to The Growth Roadmap® with some final tips to help you on your way.

Understanding that the Virgo team had intended to embark on The Growth Roadmap®, the chairperson scheduled a board meeting for three months time, when the team would need to present a clear plan to transform growth. There could be no question of rescheduling – committing time-pressed board members to a date was already an achievement. All five stages of the Roadmap had to be completed and fully communicable by the agreed date. There was no Plan B.

Having an immovable deadline had a remarkable effect on the whole Virgo team and us! Knowing that the board would be reviewing their work encouraged all members to raise their game and really engage with each stage of The Growth Roadmap®. They began seeing diagnosis, shared vision, scaling challenges and the other stages from the board's viewpoint.

If there were gaps they hurried to address them. If any of the language was sloppy or imprecise, they rewrote it. The default question became, *'how will this sound to the board and our internal team?'* They learnt to think visually, ensuring that the outputs arising from each stage were clear, concise and succinct, affording all the information needed at a glance.

They anticipated questions and became masters of link-up and flow, really nailing the connection between all five stages of The Growth Roadmap®. At the same time, they began to excel at narrative – each member was able to tell the story of where the company was now, where they would like to be and how they intended to get there. The Virgo team prepared an impressive growth strategy and summarised it on a single page (see opposite) to help tell their story.

Virgo
The Growth Roadmap® overview

① Diagnosis

- Progress has been too slow, we have lacked focus and are getting hurt on price.
- We now have the funds to scale.
- Our new Tier 1 target market requires high standards of customer service, we need to raise our game.

② Shared Vision

- We will 3X the business within 3 years by targeting Tier 1 technology companies.
- We need to change our mindset and become obsessive about customer service.
- This represents a significant cultural change in the business.

⑤ Keeping Growth on Track

- Financial assumption - if we penetrate these Tier 1 technology companies, we can move average annual revenue per client from $5m to $50m per annum.
- We will have long sales cycles to fund and the facilities are in place to do that.
- KPIs are Net Promoter Score, new accounts wins, average revenue per client, size of pipeline, number of sales people exceeding quota.

③ Strategy

- We will shift the focus to Tier 1 technology companies.
- We will require a US presence.
- Product development will focus towards meeting the needs of Tier 1 technology companies.
- We will gradually increase prices in sectors outside Tier 1 technology, to improve margins.
- We recognise that some of these sectors will find us too expensive over time.

④ Scaling Challenges

We have identified three core scaling challenges:
- Creating a compelling value proposition for Tier 1 technology companies.
- Implementing a 'land and expand' account-based sales strategy with excellent customer service.
- Focusing our product resources on delivering the optimum solution for Tier 1 technology companies.

Conclusion

A Compelling Event

When the day of the board meeting came, there was nervous anticipation in the team. This was an Event. It wasn't a meeting which would meander, ending with a lethargic A.O.B. inquiry; it was a meeting where every second counted.

The Virgo senior team had worked really hard. Their strategy, based on in-depth diagnosis, was excellent. They had identified scaling challenges and put in place the metrics to keep growth on track. Their shared vision had been repurposed and their stretch goals were now really ambitious but they were able to back up this ambition with clear direction and a set of steps to get there.

The enthusiasm of every team member was so contagious that soon the board's enthusiasm almost surpassed the team's. They were impressed with the plan for growth set out so clearly before them. They tested the plan hard, throwing up every question they could. It became a game to see if they could catch the team out, but it was evident that every eventuality was covered and that Virgo was on track to implement really ambitious growth.

The scaling challenges stage had revealed that the company would need to boost the sales team and improve customer service. This would require significant investment. But the CFO didn't need to make a pitch for the investment. It was clear to the board that the investment was linked to the delivery of the strategy, and so they were happy to support it.

The board, for their part, brought all their expertise and insight to Virgo's Growth Roadmap®. Their validation confirmed for the team that this was a solid plan. Their suggestions for improvement were insightful and further strengthened the plan. For instance, one of the board members was so taken with the dual track that she suggested another potential emerging market, which would prove to be a significant opportunity for them.

Last task: set a date and stick to it

Our experience with Virgo and many other companies like them has led us to our final recommendation for all companies working through The Growth Roadmap®. When you begin the process, set a date for completion, and stick to it.

This date doesn't necessarily have to be for a board meeting. It could be a 'town hall' meeting to unveil the work done in The Growth Roadmap® to the staff. Another client of ours, who had a workforce of 200, booked a venue for their town hall meeting and invited the whole company. They laid on drinks and refreshments and the CEO had all the learnings from the five stages of The Growth Roadmap® integrated into a booklet, which he distributed to everyone.

Booking a date three months from the start of the process is a good timeframe – it could be shorter if the team has more time to commit to the work involved. The date won't be changed, so it should be near enough to focus attention on completion, but not so near that it's unrealistic and generates stress.

Look on your deadline date as one of the metrics that ensures you finish all five stages of The Growth Roadmap® and that you continue with implementation. If you've presented your plan at board level or to the whole company, you're unlikely to shirk execution. This declaration of intent is the ultimate public weigh-in.

Catching the Growth Bug

We hope we've conveyed throughout this book that scaling plans that successfully close the growth gap have to be ambitious, realistic, clear and concise.

The value of The Growth Roadmap® is that the very process of working through the five stages instils the right disciplines and shifts mindsets. You will come to the end feeling that you have communicated your strategy clearly, that your team has a growth mindset and that you have been clear about capturing and measuring value.

Scaling will no longer be something to fear or avoid. Instead, you'll be looking forward to the next phase of transformation, to identifying and closing future growth gaps. Now you have caught the growth bug, you have a process that works, and it's one which becomes easier every time you follow it.

"It's not the destination, it's the journey that counts" as the American writer Ralph Waldo Emerson put it. He didn't mean that the voyager was uninterested in the destination. Only that all the important inward transformation happened on the journey. So when the voyager finally arrived at their destination, he had developed the capability and resilience to maximise any situation he found himself in, no matter how unexpected – and was already preparing for the next destination.

For us, it has been and remains a huge privilege to set out with growth companies on their scaling journeys. We hope you've enjoyed this book and that you're ready to set out on your own journey, open to the transformation that this will bring.

Appendices

Appendices

Appendix 1- Growth Gap Research

Background

The background research for this book consisted of understanding the reasons behind the gap between a company's current and potential performance. We call this the 'growth gap'.

Over a five year period (between 2013 and 2018), the CEOs and senior leadership teams of over 120 companies completed our growth diagnostic tool (see Appendix 2). There were over 500 senior team participants. This involved the CEO and team rating themselves on 48 quantitative statements, using a Likert Scale, and also providing qualitative responses to a set of open questions relating to performance.

All responses were treated confidentially and results for each individual company were aggregated. The extended period of time for the survey research (5 years) should remove economic uncertainty and sentiment somewhat from the responses.

In addition to the above background research on the growth gap, we engaged with the senior leadership teams of 60+ companies to refine and implement The Growth Roadmap® framework, which seeks to help close this growth gap and enable companies to scale successfully. These constitute our core Growth Roadmap® group.

Profile of Companies Researched

The indigenous Irish firms we researched and worked with typically had revenues of between €2.5m and €100m. All had between 20 and 250 employees. Each was innovation driven, either with a novel business model or technology. All had average turnover growth greater than 20% per annum over a three year period. Each had stated international growth ambitions, with customers in multiple geographies.

Participant companies ranged across a number of sectors and industries; and included both product and service examples. They were typically founder led, often investor backed, and some were family businesses. The participant company stage of development and team capability varied significantly.

The OECD defines high-growth as "All enterprises with average annualised growth greater than 20% per annum, over a three year period". We broadly used this definition when selecting our sample group for this research.

Growth Gap Findings

The high level finding was that *87% of companies felt that they were in big and growing markets, indicating the capacity for faster growth. Yet only 41% reported that shareholders were satisfied with growth rates and performance.*

We explored and investigated the growth gap under four company areas: market, product, leadership and performance.

The underlying reasons for the growth gap are dependent on each individual company situation, however clear patterns emerge with actionable insights.

Researching and documenting the growth gap served as a major input and influenced the design of our framework, The Growth Roadmap®.

From our research findings and deeper engagement with companies, we strongly believe that there is considerable potential for closing the growth gap and enabling growth firms to scale successfully, benefiting their stakeholders and communities.

The Growth Gap

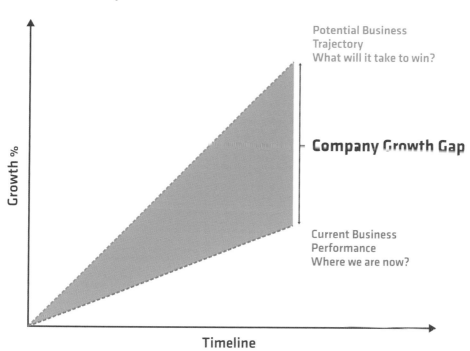

Here are the key findings, symptoms and patterns we found in the four areas; market, product, leadership and performance.

Appendices

1. Growth Gap Research Findings – Market

Market potential is generally big but lack of disciplined segmentation and compelling value propositions are contributing to the growth gap.

- **Companies are not held back by a lack of market opportunities** – 87% stated that their chosen market is big and growing and sufficient to meet their growth ambitions.

- **Many struggle to find their sweet spot customer profile** – 65% responded that they had a clearly defined profile of their ideal customer but a much smaller number felt they focused on this sweet spot – many reported time wasted trying to win or service customers who were a 'bad fit'. Analysis of this 'bad fit' revealed that ultimately companies lost money on these customers but held onto them for the ready cash they contributed.

- **Lack of sweet spot clarity results in fewer qualified sales leads** – only 47% of respondents were generating enough qualified sales leads. This lack of sales leads is often due to a capability gap, that respondents reported as falling somewhere between marketing, the emerging sales operations function and sales people themselves.

- **Companies provide valuable offerings to customers but struggle to effectively communicate the value they deliver**. Only 53% believed that prospects understand the value they deliver without face-to-face contact. Given that today's buyer is typically well-informed and buying online, the lack of clear value propositions contributes to the growth gap.

- **Lack of a clearly defined market strategy contributes to the challenge of trying to grow in multiple markets** – in response to the question – *'What has held back company growth in the past?'* – many respondents stated that the lack of a clearly stated market strategy contributed to a slowing down of business velocity and made scaling more complex.

2. Growth Gap Research Findings – Product

Product – many growth companies could do a better job at communicating their difference and delivering on their product roadmaps.

- **75% of companies surveyed believed that customers care deeply** about what separates them from the competition. However, many found it difficult to communicate what makes their offering stand out. Yet being recognised as 'trusted experts' in their chosen market was mentioned by 71% of respondents.

- **Management teams recognise the difference between growth and scale.** About 40% asserted that they had plans underway to implement the right processes at the right time. However, a consistent theme in the qualitative responses was that entrepreneurial approaches of the founder team often took priority over more scalable and repeatable approaches.

- **63% of respondents stated that they have a clearly defined product roadmap**, but only 49% felt that it had been clearly communicated to all staff. In addition, the qualitative participant responses suggested that silos often exist between marketing, sales and delivery teams.

- **61% of companies stated that their products and services were partner-ready**, indicating that many have more potential to leverage partners as a route to growth.

- **60% of companies asserted that they have repeatable processes enabling them to scale.** However, our observation is that many companies would grow much faster by implementing scalable processes earlier.

3. Growth Gap Research Findings – Leadership

Leadership teams of growth firms are trusting places but capability gaps and a lack of the right behaviours to scale contribute to the growth gap.

- **Companies trust their leadership teams –** 75% of teams stated that they have a high degree of trust in the team, a key factor in making growth happen.

- **Leadership teams often lack a concrete strategy to identify and achieve their goals –** 63% of respondents believed that their CEOs have clear and ambitious goals in place. Yet a much lower percentage 52% reported a regular review process for growth plans.

- **Leadership teams feel they have the right capabilities but need additional senior hires –** 66% of participant companies felt they had the right structure to support their growth plans.

- **In response to the question** *'what has held the company back in the past?'* **many respondents reported lack of senior leadership talent in key roles, particularly internationally.** Only 61% reported having a proven hiring process to recruit the best talent.

- **Many respondents mentioned the need for the leadership team to spend more time on people and organisational development.**

4. Growth Gap Research Findings – Performance

Performance is often below expectations and this is due to a lack of repeatable steps to win new customers.

- **Performance is frequently not meeting expectations – statistically companies perform below par on this section of the survey** – only 59% of companies stated that shareholders were satisfied with growth rates. Similarly, 55% asserted that their company did not have the funds to implement their growth plans.

- **Just over half (51%) report that they have a repeatable set of steps to win new customers – no surprise then, that only 53% are meeting sales forecasts.** Many participants highlighted the need to build stronger sales capability.

- **60% challenged the key assumptions in the business and 66% had a set of key metrics to measure progress.** However, only 55% reported that all employees understand their financial model.

- **59% of survey participants claimed that they were good at follow-on sales to existing customers.** This augers well for scaling, but based on our first-hand observations, it is likely more can be done.

- **Improved communication was reported very frequently by respondents to the question –** *'How could the performance of the company improve?'* – many cited lack of role clarity and wanting to understand more about what was happening in other company areas.

Appendix 2 – Select Strategies Growth Diagnostic Survey

Over the last ten years we've learnt a lot about helping businesses to assess where they are today. To help clients, and to assist our research, we have built a proprietary diagnostic tool.

We have developed a completely confidential online diagnostic which draws out the broader team's perspective on the business. It drills into high-level issues relating to market, product, leadership and performance and begins the process of identifying the significant areas to explore. It includes:

- Forty-eight quantitative statements that team members are asked to rate

- Five qualitative questions that point the way to a deeper understanding of where the company is today

The responses from the team members and CEO are collated and reported on separately, and any disparities between these are clearly signalled in graphic format.

Use the '5 Whys' to get beyond symptoms to root cause. Just keep digging down – asking 'why?' – until you hit the foundations. As an example, let's take Aries Solutions who we met at Stage 1:

'The length of time to close new deals is getting longer.'

Why is that?

'Prospects feel our product is difficult to understand.'

Why is that?

'Well...we didn't take time to polish off some of the screens and usability functions.'

Why didn't you?

'We assumed customers would find it easy to implement and use.'

Why would you assume that?

'Because we're engineers and it was easy for us.'

Why would you think that all customers are like you?

'Yes, it seems a gross presumption but we hardly have time to think! We're also trying to build products for other customers.'

Diagnosis: the sales velocity issue isn't the root cause; the problem is we're not prioritising, we're trying to be all things to all customers. We're not spending enough time listening to customers about how they use the product or looking at how to make the product easy to use.

Appendix 4 – Sample Business KPIs

Below is a sample set of Business KPIs that you may wish to review or choose from.

Financial KPIs

- Net profit
- Gross margin
- Revenue
- EBITDA
- Revenue growth rate
- Committed monthly recurring revenue
- Cash in bank or cash runway
- Cashflow or cash conversion cycle

Customer KPIs

- Customer satisfaction or net promoter score
- Customer acquisition cost
- Customer lifetime value
- Customer profitability
- Number of open customer support calls
- Average customer support issue resolution time

People KPIs

- Staff advocacy score
- Staff satisfaction rating
- Staff turnover
- Competency for role
- Revenue per employee

Sales KPIs

- Cost of customer acquisition
- Number of new client wins
- Sales pipeline/forecast
- Sales from new customers
- Sales from existing customers
- Number of new qualified leads
- Pipeline value

Operational KPIs

- Time to market
- Quality – customer complaints/compliments
- Time to implement/go live
- Order to cash cycle
- Product profitability
- Project profitability
- Capacity utilisation rate

Worksheets

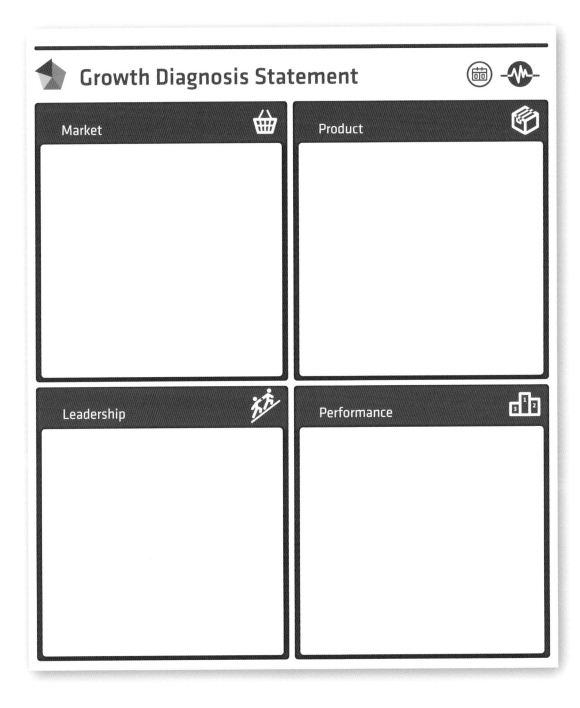

Growth Diagnosis Statement

Market

Product

Leadership

Performance

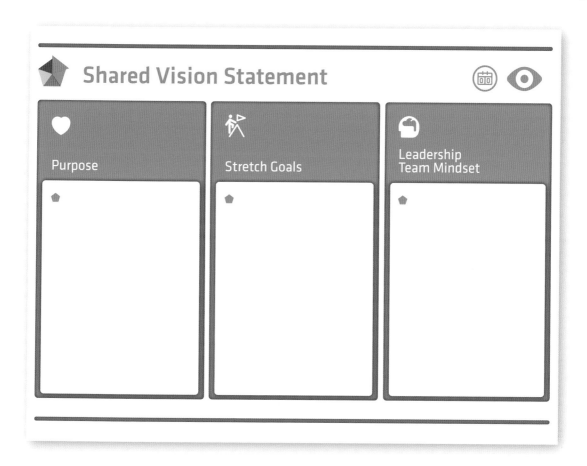

Shared Vision Statement

Purpose

Stretch Goals

Leadership Team Mindset

Strategy Statement

Industry Insight

Strategic Objectives

Product/Market Scope

Competitive Advantage

Scaling Scorecard:

Specify Company Challenge...

Objectives	Measures	Targets	Initiatives

Summary Financial Model

Summary P&L	Last year	Current year	Plan year 1	Plan year 2	Plan year 3
Revenue					
Revenue – *existing customers*					
Revenue – *new customers*					
Revenue – *new products*					
Operational Expenses					
Net Profit					
Cash					

Business KPI Model

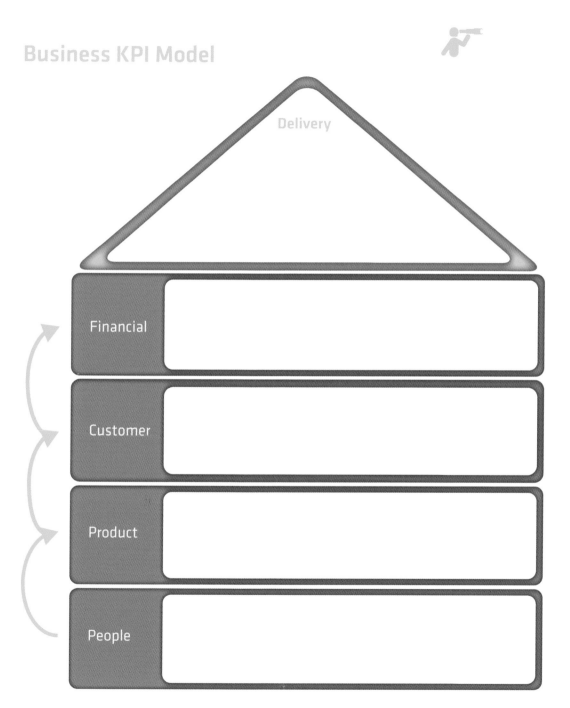

Performance Rhythm Chart

Performance Rhythm Chart

Meeting	Purpose	Attendees	Frequency	Review Focus

Glossary

Glossary

Business terms have often slightly different interpretations and this can give rise to a lack of clarity in dialogue or debate. In particular, the interpretation can vary based on industry sector, stage of development and theory. We provide here a glossary of terms we use in The Growth Roadmap®, so that readers, teams or those leading a growth transformation project, can have a quick and easy way to minimise any ambiguity about our intended meaning.

Term	Explanation
Assumptions	Business assumptions are statements that we assume to be true. Business plans are created in an environment, where the future is uncertain, but you still need to make plans and decisions.
Business KPI Model	The Business KPI Model is a visual representation, which describes business level KPIs (no more than 10) used to measure, evaluate and motivate performance. KPIs should be balanced across financial, sales, customer, product and people. The model should include both lead and lag measures.
Company Purpose	Company Purpose is the 'Why' behind your company. It goes beyond financial gain to consider at a deeper level, why your company exists? Why are your team motivated to go beyond expectations? It often strikes an emotional chord.
Competencies	Competencies are demonstrable characteristics and skills that enable performance. Distinctive ones are competencies that are unique to your company and that are superior to those in other companies. When combined, they enable the creation of competitive advantage.
Competitive Advantage	Competitive advantage is the set of attributes that enables a business to outperform its competitors. Competitive advantages arise from attributes like scale, giving leverage to offer lower costs or unique capability to deliver higher value to customers.
Competitive Advantage Worksheet	A competitive advantage worksheet is a simple visual representation of the advantage your company has over its competitors. It helps make advantages and gaps clearer, to guide and prioritise action.
Customised Solutions	Customised solutions are ones that are specially developed for specific clients. They can be contrasted with off-the-shelf productised solutions, which are designed to fit the needs of the mass market or many customers.
Diagnosis	To diagnose a business problem is to determine the source. Senior teams who can't diagnose end up treating symptoms or maybe even doing nothing at all. A good diagnosis is one which has all of your team on the same page regarding the source or root cause of your problems. It should lead to a plan to address the root cause.

Glossary

Dual Track: Exploit & Explore	The tension or trade-off between the exploration of new possibilities and the exploitation of old certainties is a strategy dilemma addressed in The Growth Roadmap®. This dual track approach is explained and the different characteristics of each track illustrated.
Execution Objectives	Execution objectives are specific targets that teams or individuals commit to. In Stage 4 we use a Scaling Scorecard approach to ensure that the results being sought are concrete and tracked through agreed KPIs and targets. We also include the initiatives and resources planned to achieve the targeted results.
Five Whys or 5 Whys (Appendix 3)	Five whys (or 5 whys) is an iterative questioning technique used to explore the cause-and-effect relationships underlying a particular problem. The primary goal of the technique is to determine the root cause of a problem by repeating the question "Why?" Each answer forms the basis of the next question.
Four Company Areas	In The Growth Roadmap®, we think of a business in a balanced way through four company areas: market, product, leadership and performance.
Growth Diagnosis Statement	The Growth Diagnosis Statement is the output from Uncover Diagnosis. It summarises on one slide the senior teams view of the current diagnosed situation, across the four company areas: market, product, leadership and performance.
Growth Gap	Growth Gap is a quantifiable gap between a company's current performance and their reasonable expectations based on overall market performance. It is often expressed in revenue or net profit, e.g. if the market is growing annually at 40% and your company is growing at just 10%, then there might be a revenue growth gap of 30%.
Industry Insight	Industry insight is developed through questions, reflection and dialogue that creates a new way of looking at the external environment. It challenges the status quo and seeks to understand the potential scenarios arising from new trends.
Initiatives	Initiatives are projects with a finite start and end date, that are intended to support strategy execution or to overcome execution challenges. Initiatives are the engine that put strategy execution into action.
Lead & Lag Measures	Lag measures are outcomes that have already happened, like revenue or profit. Whilst they are important, they are a result. Lead measures tell you if you are likely to achieve a future expected outcome. They are future predictors of performance and act like early warning systems. For example, sales performance in a given month is a lag measure. The lead measure for that sales team might have been the strength of their future prospect pipeline.
Measurable Value (see our previous publication The Business Battlecard, 2009)	Measurable value is the result of a strong customer value proposition. It can be represented by measuring how much your company helps clients to increase revenue or reduce costs.

Glossary

Measures	We use Scaling Scorecards and introduce measures and metrics that help create targets to focus on, manage and communicate expected results. Measures can be used to track progress towards meeting each objective.
Mindset	Mindset is your team's core way of thinking, based on assumptions, ambition and values. Mindset answers the question, how do we do things around here? Transformation often requires a shift in the senior leadership team to truly change or scale the business.
Performance Rhythm	Performance Rhythm is a predefined process of meetings and team interactions so that the flow of operations is as smooth as possible. It provides a structured way for teams to evaluate and communicate progress on milestones and targets at the right frequency. It brings clearer purpose and focus to your business and plans for the right people to participate in each review meeting.
Product/Market Scope	Product/Market Scope clarifies and defines the products and markets on which your business will concentrate. It defines where you are going to compete (and not going to compete). It further drills down into market segmentation, products and value proposition.
Product Roadmap	A product roadmap is a high-level visual summary that maps out the vision and direction of your product offering over time. A product roadmap communicates the why and what of your product development. It should be directly linked to and support your strategy statement.
Root Cause	Root cause is the initiating cause or chain of events leading to an outcome or effect. Using tools like the 5 Whys helps companies dig beyond symptoms and start to address the root cause.
Sales Velocity	Sales Velocity (SV) is a measurement of sales efficiency and effectiveness. SV = (no. of leads x average deal size x win rate)/ average length of buying cycle.
Scaling	Scaling means to grow or expand in an efficient, repeatable and sustainable way. It is not growth for growths sake. Scaling often involves the introduction of new processes.
Scaling Scorecard	Scaling Scorecards help translate high level strategy and scaling challenges into actions, with outputs that can be measured. They help both individuals and teams understand how they can contribute to the scaling of the business. Scaling scorecards are a powerful clarity, communication and performance assessment tool.
Select Strategies Diagnostic	This is a proprietary Select Strategies online diagnostic questionnaire, which management teams complete. It asks participants to rate their company across 48 statements in market, product, leadership and performance; and also has some follow up open questions.
Senior Leadership Team (SLT)	This is typically the senior team that participate in The Growth Roadmap® process. Sometimes depending on company size, other company managers or experts are invited to join in the process.

Glossary

Sensitivity Analysis	Sensitivity analysis is a technique, which allows the analysis of changes in assumptions used in forecasts. It is a helpful technique, used in The Growth Roadmap®, for sales, gross margin and profit forecasting.
Shared Vision	A shared vision is what your team wants to create or accomplish for your company. It is your North Star. In The Growth Roadmap®, we define shared vision as having three elements; Company Purpose, Stretch Goals and Leadership Team Mindset.
SMART Question	SMART is an acronym that can be used to help frame good questions. It stands for S(specific), M(measurable), A (achievable), R (relevant) and T (timebound).
Strategic Objectives	Strategic objectives in The Growth Roadmap® are elements of your overall strategy statement. They indicate what is critical or important in your organisational strategy and are communicated clearly in the form of measurable primary objectives, like revenue and profit in a short timeframe 12–18 months, which makes sense in the context of growth firms.
Strategy	We define strategy as a high level step to operationalise and achieve your shared vision. Due to the uncertain nature of the environment for growth firms, we define strategy in short time periods, like 12–18 months and encourage continual review. We use a dual track of exploit and explore and provide a strategy statement based on leadership insight, product/market choices and creation of competitive advantage.
Stretch Goals	Stretch goals involve radical expectations that go beyond current capabilities and performance. They should be small in number and contribute to a 3-year shared vision.
Summary Financial Model	The summary financial model is a high level model which translates the overall strategy into a set of assumptions, upon which 3-year financial forecasts are based. It also includes some key performance trend ratios. The summary financial model (typically 5–10 rows) should tell the story of the strategy using financial language that your senior team understand.
Sweet Spot (see our previous publication The Business Battlecard, 2009)	Sweet spot is a golf term alluding to the favoured spot on the clubface, where contact with the ball feels best. We use it to describe the profile of that segment of customers that your product suits best e.g. they have a problem to solve or job to be done, that your company addresses really well.
Targets	The Growth Roadmap® sets targets to achieve for each Execution Objective in the Scaling Scorecard. These targets help both individuals and teams evaluate and measure progress performance. They help teams learn faster, make corrective actions and celebrate success.

Glossary

The Growth Roadmap®	The Growth Roadmap® describes the overall framework for scaling growth. It consists of 5 stages: 1. Uncover Diagnosis; 2. Commit to a Shared Vision; 3. Select the Right Strategy; 4. Overcome Scaling Challenges; 5. Keep Growth on Track.
Transformation	We define transformation as fundamentally changing processes, people and technology across a business, to close the 'growth gap and scale successfully'.
Value Proposition	Value proposition describes what value a customer will receive from buying your product. We encourage clients to try to quantify this value in a financial or measurable way, in what we call 'measurable value'. This can be categorised into how much you make or save a customer.